THE
GARDEN
SOURCE

THE GARDEN SOURCE

Inspirational Design Ideas for Gardens and Landscapes

Andrea Jones

Foreword by
James van Sweden

To Mum, with love and thanks.
It must have been your passion for gardening that somehow started me off on this journey of garden photography. Happy memories of playing in the maze of your little box hedges as a small child with you, Dad and Brett. Enjoying the apples from the orchard and sniffing the scented flowers in the rose garden. I hope you will enjoy these pages and think I have been doing something useful with my time in recent years – not just gallivanting around the world!

Acknowledgments

Special thanks to all the garden owners, designers, and gardeners who have provided me with the subject matter for my photography over the years. Your kindness, cooperation, and generosity continues to be hugely appreciated.

To Noel Kingsbury for his support and encouragement with this and so many projects. All staff and friends at Chanticleer Gardens in Pennsylvania for their continued support and inspiration over the years; especially Jonathan Wright who has so enthusiastically assisted me with garden advice. Also Mrs Pat Bader who has helped me find my feet – and many wonderful gardens in the United States.

Enormous thanks to my husband, Alasdair Currie, not only for endless scanning and digital processing (often late into the night), helping to prepare images and researching captions, but also for his continual support.

Lastly, sincere thanks to Mark Fletcher and Damian Jaques who came up with the idea for this book and patiently led and cajoled me through the process of making it, whilst designing and editing its pages meticulously.

First published in the United States of America in 2012 by
Rizzoli International Publications, Inc.
300 Park Avenue South
New York, NY 10010
www.rizzoliusa.com

Originally published in the United Kingdom in 2011 by
Eight Books Limited
18 Elwin Street
London E2 7BU
www.8books.co.uk

Text and design © 2011 Eight Books Limited
Photographs © 2011 Andrea Jones

Design: Damian Jaques
Editorial: Mark Fletcher
Picture research: Alasdair Currie

2012 2013 2014 2015 / 10 9 8 7 6 5 4 3 2 1

ISBN: 978-0-8478-3759-5

Library of Congress Control Number: 2011933612

Printed in China

The publishers have done their best to ensure the accuracy of all the information in *The Garden Source* and cannot accept responsibility for any inconvenience or loss caused as a result of the information contained in this book.

PREVIOUS PAGE: "Reflexions Colorees", International Garden Festival, Jardin de Metis/Reford Gardens, Quebec, Canada. Design: Hal Ingberg

CONTENTS

FOREWORD

The opportunity to delve into Andrea Jones' *The Garden Source* arrives for me at an opportune time – cold and dreary January. Looking at this very fine collection of photography is an armchair vacation of sorts, and while it may not cure the seasonal affective disorder to which humankind seems prone, I can guarantee that the hours spent with this lovely book will have a salubrious effect on every reader/viewer.

Just as daffodils became a mental resource for Wordsworth, so books like Andrea's serve to comfort the gardener mired in "vacant or in pensive mood". True, we may never enjoy the temperate climate or the inspiring sites available to some of the gardeners featured here; nonetheless there is something to be gleaned from all of these images, elements that can be translated from one garden clime or garden style to another without losing anything in the process.

Consider, for example, the lovely and somewhat unexpected juxtaposition of casual and sprightly tulips with gleaming modern sculpture at the start of the book on pages 22-23. It reminds me, yes, of spring's imminent return but also encourages reflection on the value of sculpture in the garden. Sculpture can serve as a destination at the end of the path, provide a focal point, offer a necessary element of contrast, or insert a sudden jolt of pure emotion into a garden setting. And, it leads me to consider how the shifting light and seasonal change provided by a garden – as opposed to a gallery – vivify a sculpture, highlighting various aspects of a work, inviting people to project their own moods.

The very simple, even primal spheres by Grace Knowlton so beautifully captured here by Andrea in Oehme van Sweden's garden at Cornerstone, Sonoma, California (opposite and page 228), is perhaps the simplest illustration of these principles. Over the years, I've owned and enjoyed several of Knowlton's spheres; I used them to amazing effect in my small garden in Georgetown and now they occupy both interior and exterior spaces at my country home on Maryland's Eastern shore. I've also placed them in the gardens of many clients, including Knowlton's own garden. She, of course, moves and regroups them while a typical client might not feel so free to experiment (an unfortunate fact).

Sculpture has a galvanizing effect on a garden. As readers turn the pages of Andrea's book they will see this point writ large and small. Sculpture, broadly defined, may be a specific and official "work of art" or a compelling gate or gazebo that provides a focal point while adding to the interplay between the garden "proper" (i.e. the plants and their arrangement) and the architectural elements. Looking through this book, you will see that fact illustrated again and again.

But let's not forget the details! Landscape architects use this word to describe the specific elements of paths, patios, pergolas and much more. Those details and the potential richness they bring to a landscape are catalogued here as perhaps never before. In this sense, Andrea provides a fabulous resource and reference volume – one that will be drawn upon for inspiration by gardeners and landscape architects alike.

Consider this book not only as a source of ideas for your garden, but also as a means of learning from this gifted photographer. In so doing you will gain a different perspective on your landscape. With Andrea's help you will see your own garden with new eyes. I've spent many happy hours with this book and I know you will, too.

James van Sweden

RIGHT: "The Garden of Contrasts", Cornerstone Festival of Gardens, Sonoma, CA, USA. Design: James van Sweden and Sheila Brady.

INTRODUCTION

There is nothing quite like visiting gardens to get ideas for designing your own.
The range of styles in which gardens have been created is phenomenal and any opportunity to visit a new one should not be missed. As a garden photographer I have had more opportunities than most to visit not just gardens open to the public, but also some very private gardens. I have returned from so many trips with my mind buzzing full of ideas and my car brimming full of plants. Plants and ideas that have often enthusiastically been shared.

So this book is an opportunity to give back and share some experiences I have been lucky enough to enjoy by making available a selection of photographs I have taken in those gardens. I hope this will be useful and inspirational to future designers. And I hope through this book to share some of the ideas I have encountered on my journey as a photographer and give the reader inspiration for their own garden (or their clients').

I first photographed gardens in the early 1990s when a recession was in full flow. This was not perhaps the best time to start on a new specialist direction to any photographic career, but as it happened the economic cutbacks made people think more about what they could do with their own backyards. Some simply wanted to justify staying at home so as to preclude any unnecessary spending, others wanted to make a more attractive space or grow their own vegetables. The rest, understandably, wanted to improve the saleability of their property.

The age of the makeover emerged and TV shows featured celebrity gardeners who painted trellises in greeny-blue and created water features from recycled washing machines – all manner of imaginative makeshift tricks. Popular TV shows may not have featured the most sophisticated of designs, but they certainly renewed public interest and appreciation of garden design.

During this period I was commissioned to take the photographs for a book accompanying the first television series of "Garden Doctors" for Channel 4 in England with the young designers Dan Pearson and Steve Bradley. This gave me my initial insight into how a designer can transform a space from start to finish. The gardens were nearly all domestic, ranging from the balconies of a block of flats in South London to a shady garden bordering a woodland in Buckinghamshire, England.

RIGHT: Hermannshof, Germany

BELOW: "Merrill Lynch Garden", RHS Chelsea Flower Show 2004, London, UK. Design: Dan Pearson

ABOVE: Fazenda Marambaia, formerly the Odette Monteiro Residence, Petropolis, Brazil. Design: Burle Marx and Haruyoshi Ono

I looked on as the designers maximized vertical space by making concrete planters around supports at the base of the apartment block, twirled creeping plants up and around iron railings, and planted window boxes. Where there was little light in the shady garden they used what they had to the best advantage: light-coloured gravel to reflect any stray trickles of sunlight and shade-tolerant plants to fill the borders. Grids were laid on the lawn to hoodwink the eyes using tricks of perspective and to give advantageous sightlines from the kitchen window of the house. Clever ways were invented to get the garden visitor from A to B by means of rustic steps, canopied walkways, and curved mosaic paths.

Today, design questions continue to be asked of garden owners, designers, and landscape architects. How do you give shared owners a degree of privacy in a community garden? How do you screen off the kids' football pitch from the dining room window? How do you connect a swimming pool with the landscape so that it appears to float into the hills? How do you shade a south-facing garden so you can enjoy sitting in it at any time of day? How do you join levels of terraced garden seamlessly and stylishly? The questions are endless.

Through my work as a garden photographer I have been fortunate enough to travel all over the world visiting wonderful gardens by leading designers, many of which are reproduced on these pages. I first began my work in Britain. The British are known for their love of gardens and have been at the forefront of garden design and landscape architecture for centuries – diverse characters such as Lancelot "Capability" Brown, Humphry Repton, Edwin Lutyens, Margery Fish, and more recently, the flamboyant figure of Christopher Lloyd, helped develop a reputation of great British style in gardening. This was achieved, in some cases, by reorganizing the landscape of vast estates, giving a sense of proportion by adding structural bones to plots of land, and by planting them with unexpected combinations of plants (occasionally with controversial clashes of colour).

Partnerships such as that of Gertrude Jekyll and Edwin Lutyens blossomed and even Vita Sackville-West was known to credit her husband Harold Nicolson with laying out the formality of the design at Sissinghurst. The Canadian designers, Sandra and Nori Pope, made a huge impact on Britain's garden styles working with colour in the garden of Hadspen. Beth Chatto began working on her gardens in 1960 when the site was an overgrown wasteland. Beth and her late husband, Andrew Chatto, used their dry and damp soils in both sun and shade, putting into practice the underlying principles of what is now referred to as "ecological gardening". A small team at Sheffield University have since taken this a step further by using ecological techniques in the urban landscape.

In Italy I have photographed masterpieces of garden design at Villa Lante in Bagnaia and Villa D'Este in Tivoli, both of which use water playfully on a grand scale. Although tricky to photograph, they are both breathtakingly magnificent. At Villandry in France (page 207) I have a magical memory of formal gardens – vegetables and ornamental plants given equal precedence in a razor-sharp formality.

Prolific garden writer Dr. Noel Kingsbury, chiefly known for promoting naturalistic and sustainable planting design, introduced me to another world of horticultural culture. We have regularly worked together over the last ten years, including in Germany and the Netherlands. At Hermannshof (page 9) I found one of my all-time favourite public gardens, a very painterly mass of perennials, their colours and textures blending gently. In Holland, renowned plantsman Piet Oudolf permitted me to photograph the plants and gardens at his home in Hummelo (page 107) while he was still experimenting with new planting ideas.

Noel also introduced me to the work of Roberto Burle Marx, known as the "true inventor of the Modern Garden". In the late 1920s Burle Marx studied painting in Berlin, Germany, where he often visited the greenhouses of the Dahlem Botanic Garden. It was here that he first appreciated the beauty of the tropical plants and the flora of his native Brazil. Soon after returning home he embarked on his first landscape architecture projects developing a style using indigenous plants in broad brushstrokes across gardens around Rio and beyond (opposite and page 286). His work in turn has inspired such leading figures in American garden design as James van Sweden and his German partner Wolfgang Oehme who together revolutionized landscape architecture and created the "New American Garden" style in the 1980s (page 228). Like Burle Marx they brought a musical rhythm to planting using native American herbaceous perennials and ornamental grasses as measured repetitive notes in their garden orchestrations.

The intricate and innovative landscape designs produced by the creative team at Reed Hilderbrand in the United States have been a huge source of inspiration for me. Their analytical, yet sensitive, approach with meticulous delivery to every project has made photographing their work a dream, from the curvaceous steel fencing of the Hither Lane project on Long Island (page 11) to the winding boardwalk through swamp in Massachusetts (page 57). It was at the gently sloping landscaped stone terraces of the Arnold Arboretum (page 244) that I learned to accentuate in my photographs the subtle nuances of gradients designed to be unnoticed; a new challenge for me and from which I gained a better understanding of landscape architecture.

My knowledge of Japanese gardens was mostly based on Western interpretations until I visited Japan for myself and I learned to appreciate the art of landscape architect Fumiaki Takano and his team. Japanese garden design is a vast subject, but the common western perception is of a raked gravel Zen garden where one must not tread. Mr. Takano and his team unexpectedly embrace interaction between man and nature and have created play parks for children and adults with an exceptional sense of fun and exploration. Climbing nets, marshmallow trampolines, and dragon heads all formed part of the fantasy world I encountered at Showa Kinen Park near Tokyo (page 200).

I have also travelled in Asia with the esteemed plant hunters Sue and Bleddyn Wynn-Jones of Crûg Farm. They introduced me to the excitement of discovering new plants in the field and bringing them into cultivation – seeds brought back from the remotest areas later to be grown and reproduced. Some of these new plants are now displayed in show gardens, such as those at the Chelsea Flower Show in London and in cutting-edge private gardens in mainland Europe.

Over time many influential and successful individual garden designers and cultures from different continents have evolved their own styles and philosophies which, as travel and communication have become easier, have cross-fertilized around the world. Ideas borrowed from one continent have often translated into another making the possibilities in garden design more and more exciting.

Gardens have not only changed through history, but also they have helped make history. Tranquillity has been found in them, battles have been fought in them, treaties have been signed, romances have blossomed. Over the centuries children have played in them, scientific discoveries have been made in them, much food consumed and plenty of wine drunk in them. Each and every garden has evolved completely differently depending on the landscape in which it was created in and the differing elements – the climate, the taste, the wealth, and sometimes the politics of the owner, the availability of materials, plants, and crucially, the water supply. Surely there can never be a single right answer to any design question.

Throughout history there have been different problems to solve whilst designing outdoor spaces. This book is but a small snapshot of some of the best garden solutions from around the world. The chapters are broken down into four sections – Connect, Divide, Space, and Style – which I believe will make it simple to use. Ultimately, I hope that this book will inspire new garden designs which will enrich people's lives.

CONNECT

Just as a corridor in a dwelling joins one room to another, so garden areas need to be connected by various means, not only by physically connecting one area to another, but also by bonding the outdoor life together using devices that make the garden more interesting and pleasurable.

Outdoor areas need access to each other and sometimes distance between them. Getting from one to another can be made an enjoyable part of the whole garden experience: the refreshing early morning walk up a path to a greenhouse to see how seedlings are coming along; listening to the birds singing and the sight of early morning dew on the lawn; ambling along a gently-lit path from a shed back to one's house when the tools have been put away and the light is fading. These short, but exquisite, moments can be enhanced to maximize our precious time in our outdoor spaces.

I once photographed a project in Ireland, a private seaside garden in the North, where intriguing curvaceous paths had been created. This had been achieved not by deliberate design or mathematics, but by the "deer tracks" of children scampering up and down the slope between the seashore and the kitchen. Rather than scolding the children and making them walk up the existing path, the owner (their grandmother) constructed small steps winding through the steep perennial borders carefully following the children's paths, so the scampering could continue to be enjoyed.

Should we look from the inside, out onto a garden or from the outside in? Different cultures have made us aware of their viewpoints. The Chinese famously framed natural vistas looking out of the garden area; the Japanese looked more closely from their houses at the smaller spaces surrounding them. Indeed, the Japanese are known for introducing smaller, controlled elements of nature to represent the natural world outside and to give a feeling of softness and strength through their solidity and placing.

Devices such as windows and moongates can be used to help connect to the landscape and encourage the viewer to pause for a transition into a new space. Reflections in a pool can link the outside world to a domestic situation and vice versa. Equally swathes of plants can mimic the natural landscape in the distance whilst maintaining control over a smaller environment.

The distance and style of the connection between areas will dictate the way you visit a garden and the speed you pass through it. For instance, a winding path through a pergola of fragrant roses may encourage a contemplative walk during which you can smell the scent of flowers. Whereas if the path is streamlined and direct it can make you move swiftly to avoid unsightly areas or divert your eyes from the neighbours' refuse by providing an alternate focus. A gate will make you stop to open it; graduated steps will allow you to keep an even pace and a steady viewpoint.

Connecting areas set the pace – slowing things to a stroll to give you time to think or speeding up your gait to get you to another area without distraction. These connecting elements would seem to need careful consideration when planning a garden design.

ABOVE: A Corten steel archway leads to a lawn cut into a circular island by a rill surrounded by deciduous woodland. *The Hidden Gardens, Glasgow, Scotland. Design: nva organisation and City Design Cooperative*

LEFT: This spiral lawn design is based on the Golden Section. The centre is raised and the perimeter a curving brick wall. Within its boundaries are a flowering herbaceous perennial border, water feature, deck, boardwalk, and meadow/woodland area. *Merril Lynch Garden, RHS Chelsea Flower Show 2003. Design: Xa Tollemache*

ABOVE: This striped lawn creates an elegant carpet for the paved patio with urns planted with *Cordyline* (cabbage palms), *Phormium* (New Zealand flax), and succulents. *The Terrace Garden, Chanticleer Garden, Pennsylvania, USA. Design: Dan Benarcik*

RIGHT: The design of this large lawn with mature deciduous trees and shrub borders is based on a modern aesthetic, but respects the history of the site's riparian drainage pattern on the east side of the Hudson. *Irvington, NY, USA. Design: Reed Hilderbrand*

ABOVE: Snow-covered "Tapis vert" sculpted mown lawn connects to wide views of the English countryside. *Sholebroke Lodge, Northamptonshire, England. Design: Owner, Deirdre Fenwick*

LEFT: Crisscross mown lawn with an ornamental *Prunus* (cherry) tree. *Holywell Hall, Lincolnshire, England. Design: Bunny Guinness*

PAGE RIGHT
TOP LEFT: Stepped lawn, concrete edging, and metal-mesh grid on a contemporary roof garden. *Jardin Atlantique, Gare Montparnasse, Paris, France. Design: Francois Brun and Michel Pena*

TOP RIGHT: This contemporary show garden features a limestone bath planted with turf to create a miniature lawn. *"Marks and Spencer Cut Grass Garden", RHS Chelsea Flower Show 2000. Design: Stephen Woodhams*

RIGHT: Long granite paving slabs are embedded through this lawn. *Cambridge, MA, USA. Design: Reed Hilderbrand*

FAR RIGHT: This coastal garden has a permeable concrete and grass driveway bordered by drought-tolerant plants, including *Callistemon citrinus* (bottlebrush) and *Euphorbia* (spurge). *Santa Barbara, CA, USA. Design: Isabelle Greene*

ABOVE: A polished steel cascade water feature is the centrepiece of this lawn planted with tulips and dotted with *Taxus baccata* (English yew). It is surrounded by borders of herbaceous perennials within a stone wall. *Kislingbury, Northamptonshire, England. Design: James Alexander-Sinclair*

LEFT: Blue gravel chippings patterned by pebbles is an alternative way to decorate a smaller space. *Warren Farm Centre's "The Essence of Life" Courtyard Garden, RHS Chelsea Flower Show 2000. Design: Rosamond Page*

BELOW LEFT: Several layers of coloured gravel feature in this drought-tolerant themed show garden. Planting includes *Allium karataviense, Dasylirion acrotrichum,* and *Asphodeline lutea.* "Kelly's Creek", *RHS Chelsea Flower Show 2002. Design: Alison Wear and Miranda Melville*

BELOW RIGHT: Red bricks are placed to accentuate the curves in a pebble path that winds through this garden. *The Madoo Conservancy, Sagaponack, Long Island, NY, USA. Design: Robert Dash*

PAGE RIGHT
TOP LEFT: Coloured cast rendered paving slabs boldly punctuate the pebbles along the path in this plantsman's garden. *Windcliff, Bainbridge Island, WA, USA. Design: Daniel J. Hinkley and Robert Jones*

TOP MIDDLE: Neatly raked gravel paths provide the base for an installation garden, "Core Sample", that uses translucent core samples from the local area. The poles are surrounded by mounds of ornamental grasses. *International Garden Festival, Jardin de Metis/Reford Gardens, Quebec, Canada. Design: Pete and Alissa North*

TOP RIGHT: Gravel gives a seaside feel to this eating area for two. A faded red metal table and chairs alongside the red foliage of a Japanese maple continue the coastal theme. *Ardentinny, Argyllshire, Scotland. Design: Owners, Barry and Freda Waldapfel*

RIGHT: A gravel path and stone paving surround a pool in the White Work Garden (part of a contemporary garden design that tells the story of alchemists' attempts to turn lead into gold). Planting includes *Rosa* 'Iceberg' (or 'Fée de Neiges'), gaura, and *Miscanthus sinensis. Le Jardin de L'Alchimiste, Eygalieres en Provence, France. Design: Arnaud Maurières and Éric Ossart*

FAR RIGHT: *Buxus sempervirens* balls on contrasting gravel. *The Madoo Conservancy, Sagaponack, Long Island, NY, USA. Design: Owner, Robert Dash*

LEFT TO RIGHT:
> Cobble stones and moss
> Porous circular paving design with stone and brick. *Design: Marcus de la Fleur*
> Slate tiles with contrasting grout
> Gravel chippings
> Chipped slate

LEFT: Contrasting tiled stone paving and wooden boardwalk create the walkways through this small minimalist garden. A chunky wooden bench, stone fountain, pond, and wooden slatted fencing all create a restful area. Planting in the herbaceous perennial borders includes *Stipa tenuissima*, astelia, and *Echinacea* (cone flower). *RHS Wisley, Surrey, England. Design: Andy Sturgeon*

LEFT BELOW: In this contemporary potager show garden, "Pomme de Parterre", wooden boardwalks and vegetable beds surround a wood shed. Planting includes potato varieties, *Tropaeolum majus*, and *Calendula officinalis* (pot marigold). *International Garden Festival, Jardin de Métis/Reford Gardens, Quebec, Canada. Design: Angela Larocci, Claire Ironside, and David K. Ross*

RIGHT TOP: A wooden boardwalk under a pergola in a secluded suburban garden. The backdrop is woven reed screening next to a pond with graded pebble shore. Planting includes shade-loving plants such as *Acer* (maple), *Dicksonia antarctica* (Tasmanian tree fern), and hosta. *Essex, England. Design: Owners Mr. and Mrs. Michael Richards*

RIGHT MIDDLE: Green oak deck, terrazzo bench seating, and woven wicker cushions surround a reflecting pool. Planting includes *Iris pseudacorus*, coppiced *Salix* (willow), and *Hemerocallis* (daylily). *"Merrill Lynch Garden", RHS Chelsea Flower Show 2004. Design: Dan Pearson*

RIGHT: A wooden deck and woven wicker screen surround a mosaic-tiled swimming pool decorated with containers of aloes. *Spalding, Lincolnshire, England. Design: Owners, Freddy Honnor and Maria Stamp*

FAR RIGHT: Here a raised wooden deck makes a platform for a relaxed seating and eating area. Driftwood furniture and patio furniture enhance the coastal look of this example of "New American Garden" style. *Chesapeake Bay, Maryland, USA. Design: Owner, James van Sweden*

LEFT: A wooden deck with coloured concrete paving is divided by strips of grass leading to an evergreen oak tree. *Bay Area, San Francisco, CA, USA. Design: Topher Delaney*

BELOW: Low-maintenance city rooftop garden. This irregular-shaped wooden deck is surrounded by gravel. Windproof planting includes *Phormium* (New Zealand flax), tulips, and *Festuca glauca* (blue fescue) in stainless steel containers. *The Piper Building, Fulham, London, England. Planting design: Matt Vincent*

BOTTOM: This simple linear wooden deck with steps, shady pergola, and container planting makes a suburban family garden that is easy to maintain. *Derby, Derbyshire, England. Design and landscaping: Paul Thompson and Ann-Marie Powell*

RIGHT: A wooden deck leads into a country cottage garden. Tile paving, a rustic metal table with *objets trouvé*, and a bench are surrounded by wisteria. *Spalding, Lincolnshire, England. Design: Owners, Freddy Honnor and Maria Stamp*

FAR RIGHT: This low-maintenance drought-tolerant garden features a wooden deck, raised boardwalk, pebble beds, and railway sleeper (railroad tie) raised beds containing architectural plants. *London, England. Design: Matt Vincent*

RIGHT: Here a spiral wooden boardwalk in natural woodland creates a running space for children in the middle of which is a willow woven tepee. *Wiltshire, England. Design: James and Helen Dooley*

FAR RIGHT: In this Japanese-style public garden a wooden boardwalk and upright posts zig zag through a sea of raked gravel, ferns, and natural deciduous woodland. *Ronnerby, Sweden. Design: Sven Ingvar Anderssen*

ABOVE: Contemporary cottage-style garden with a wooden jetty and metal steps lead down to the lawn where *Fagus sylvatica* (beech) columns punctuate the grass. Stone paving and a gravel path connect herbaceous perennial borders. *Blackpitts Farm, Towcester, Northamptonshire, England. Design: Owner, James Alexander-Sinclair*

FAR LEFT: Summerhouse with wooden chairs looking out onto a lawn with large borders of ornamental grasses and perennials. *Landenberg, PA, USA. Design: Owners, Rick Darke and Melinda Zoehrer*

LEFT: Stepped multi-platform wooden deck with container planting. Planting includes succulents such as agave, aloe, and *Aeonium arboreum* var. *atropurpureum* 'Schwarzkopf'. *Former Heronswood Nursery, Kingston, WA, USA. Design: Former owners, Daniel J. Hinkley and Robert Jones*

ABOVE: Decking with inset lights and lamps leads to a raised platform with outdoor lounge-style seating. Uplit planting includes *Trachycarpus fortunei* (Chusan palm, windmill palm). The overall effect is of an architectural evergreen jungle garden. *Norwich, Norfolk, England. Design: Owner, Jon Kelf*

ABOVE: Contemporary outdoor room for tropical climates with lounge-style seating. Circles in the pergola roof link to the circular drinks table. Viewed from the kitchen area you can see through the window in the slatted screen walls semi-tropical planting such as banana and bamboo. *Trailfinders Australian Garden, RHS Chelsea Flower Show 2010. Design: Scott Wynd*

Slatted wooden fence and gate connect this path from the drive to a residential garden. The path is made of granite paving slabs; planting includes *Vinca* (periwinkle) and *Corylus avellana* (hazel) for height. *Cambridge, MA, USA. Design: Reed Hilderbrand*

Black *Ophiopogon planiscapus* 'Nigrescens' (lilyturf) outline this Japanese-style garden path. Roughcast concrete paving slabs with stone cobbles lead to a wooden entrance gateway. *Bloedel Reserve, Bainbridge Island, WA, USA. Design: Prentice and Virginia Bloedel, Fujitaro Kubota*

Modernist garden landscape with stone paving slabs leading directly through the lawn to the house. Planting includes magnolias and *Hedera* (ivy) as ground cover. Photographed 1/08/2008. *Indianapolis Museum of Art Miller House and Garden, Columbus, IN, USA. Design: Dan Kiley*

Lush plantsman's garden with cast and dyed concrete paving and pebbles. Borders planted with shrubs and herbaceous perennials include euphorbia and fuchsia. *Windcliff, Bainbridge Island, WA, USA. Design: Daniel J. Hinkley and Robert Jones*

FAR LEFT: Stone paving slabs are inset into the lawn in this modern-style landscaped garden bordered with herbaceous perennials and evergreen hedges. *Alchemilla mollis* (lady's mantle) and hydrangea line the path. *Hither Lane, The Hamptons, Long Island, NY, USA. Design: Reed Hilderbrand*

LEFT: Lawn interrupted by irregular natural stone paving slabs lead to a roughcast concrete patio in this relaxing modern coastal garden. Climbers include bougainvillea. *Santa Barbara, CA, USA. Design: Isabelle Greene*

Stone paving slab path lined with *Alchemilla mollis* (lady's mantle), hardy geranium, and *Pulmonaria* (lungwort). Stone troughs, a cast iron street lamp, wooden porch, and pergola add to the cottage garden style. *Bourne, Lincolnshire, England. Design: Owners, Mr. and Mrs. Ivan Hall*

Brick and cobble path, buxus hedging, arching stone walls, and pollarded trees create "The Drunkard's Walk", "Soliton Gate". *The Garden of Cosmic Speculation, Dumfries and Galloway, Scotland. Design: Owners, Charles Jencks and Maggie Keswick*

Pathway of porous brick paving edged by lawn and prairie planting border. Environmentally sustainable garden using recycled materials and native planting. *Elmhurst, IL, USA. Design: Marcus de la Fleur*

FAR LEFT: An edged gravel path leads to a house through a wooden gate with hydrangea shrub varieties planted in bark-mulched borders in the Hydrangeum Living Collection. *Belgian Hydrangea Society Collection and Display Garden, Destelbergen, Ghent, Belgium. Design: Belgian Hydrangea Society*

LEFT: A graded pebble path leads through this evergreen garden to a town house and conservatory. Planting includes flowering magnolia, *Buxus sempervirens*, *Laurus nobilis*, *Cupressus* (cypress) varieties, and mahonia. *Twickenham, Surrey, England. Design: Ian Sidaway*

ABOVE LEFT: Cast concrete slab and pebble paving in a contemporary Japanese-style show garden. *"The Garden of Visceral Serenity", Cornerstone Gardens, Sonoma, CA, USA. Design: Yoji Sasaki*

ABOVE RIGHT: Perfectly placed pebbles create this swirling mosaic path bordered with brightly coloured flowering herbaceous perennial borders. Planting includes *Hemerocallis* (daylily), geum, and *Nepeta* (catmint). *The Cancer Research UK Life Garden, RHS Chelsea Flower Show 2004. Design: Jane Hudson and Erik de Maeijer*

LEFT: A simple sweeping lawn path shows off spring borders in this town garden. *Lancaster, Lancashire, England. Design: David Redmore*

PAGE RIGHT
ABOVE RIGHT: Granite setts steer a curved path through borders of architectural evergreen plants, including *Cordyline* (cabbage palm), astelia, *Trachycarpus fortunei* (windmill palm), and *Phormium* (New Zealand flax). *Norwich, Norfolk, England. Design: Owner, Jon Kelf*

RIGHT: Wooden-edged trays of pebbles set in concrete with rope and wooden poles for hand rails. *"Lip na Cloiche", Isle of Mull, Scotland. Design: Owner, Lucy Mackenzie Panizzon*

FAR RIGHT: Stone paths of different textured pebbles and rock cross over each other to run under a rustic pergola made of tree branches. *Madeira Botanical Garden, Portugal. Design: Madeira Regional Government*

BELOW: Mature *Fagus sylvatica* (beech) clipped hedge with gateway leads through an avenue of trees to an urn at the furthest point in this historic topiary garden. *Levens Hall, Kendal, Cumbria, England*

BELOW LEFT: This stone archway and solid stone path with steps leads to a glistening sea view. The avenue beyond includes *Trachycarpus fortunei* (chusan palm) with underplanting of osteospermum. *Lamorran House, St. Mawes, Cornwall, England. Design: Owner, Robert Dudley-Cooke*

BELOW MIDDLE: Metal pergolas in this formal Victorian potager walled garden are covered in vines. The brick paving path is dotted with terracotta urns filled with petunias and lined with boxwood hedging. *Titsey Place, Oxted, Surrey, England. Design: Historic owners; the Leveson Gower family. Titsey Place is currently run by the Titsey Foundation.*

BELOW RIGHT: A gravel path leads through this Arts & Crafts-style cottage garden to the back entrance of the house through an archway clad with *Hedera* (ivy). Planting alongside the path includes geranium, *Nepeta* (catmint), *Buxus sempervirens*, and rose climbers. *Hertfordshire, England. Design: Owner, Kim Wilde*

CLOCKWISE FROM TOP LEFT:
A stone archway leads the eyes to an antique ceramic urn flanked by columnar *Cupressus* (cypress) trees in this old Mediterranean terrace garden in the Alpes-Maritimes. *Menton, Provence, France. Design and restoration: Owner, William Waterfield*

Here a painted wooden archway with metal gate leads to a gravel path and low *Buxus sempervirens* hedge with a stone figure as a focal point. *Bourne, Lincolnshire, England. Design: Owners, Ivan and Sadie Hall*

Brick walls and painted wooden gateway frame a view of the house. Low *Buxus sempervirens* hedge and clipped *Carpinus betulus* (hornbeam) topiary allée create an Arts & Crafts-style garden. *Bourne, Lincolnshire, England. Design: Owners, Ivan and Sadie Hall*

The gravel and brick-edged path leads the eye into a continuous vision of lush foliage through this country garden. A metal pergola runs through rose borders dotted with shrubs and conifers. *Richards Castle, Shropshire, England. Design: Owner, Jennie Goodrich*

FAR LEFT: A circular stone window leads the eye to a pool with seating. The garden uses native wild Irish/British common plants. *Tearmann Sí — A Celtic Sanctuary, RHS Chelsea Flower Show 2002. Design: Mary Reynolds*

LEFT TOP: Metal drainage pipe leads to borders of herbaceous perennial plants. *"Rise", Cornerstone Festival of Gardens, Sonoma, CA, USA. Design: David McCrory and Roger Raiche*

LEFT MIDDLE: A brick moongate opens the view to the house at Naumkeag, *Stockbridge, MA, USA. Design: Fletcher Steele and Miss Mabel Choate*

LEFT BOTTOM: This rectangular cut-out looks through to an enclosed Japanese-style rock and moss garden. *Portland, OR, USA. Design: Owners, Norm Kalbfleisch and Neil Matteucci*

ABOVE: This lime-rendered wall with window of handmade sculptural glass peaks into the garden. Plants include *Malus* (apple) tree, peony, and *Anthriscus sylvestris* (cow parsley). *"The Lladro Garden", RHS Chelsea Flower Show 2003. Design: Chris Moss and Fiona Lawrenson*

ABOVE LEFT: An avenue of catalpa trees overhangs a brick pathway and leads to a patio with mesh seat and bronze mouse sculpture. Planting includes *Buxus sempervirens* ball topiary, pachysandra ground cover, *Digitalis* (foxglove), and *Helleborus* (hellebores). *Oceanico Garden, RHS Chelsea Flower Show 2008. Design: Diarmuid Gavin and Sir Terence Conran*

LEFT: This allée of *Gleditsia triacanthos* (honey locust) is accentuated by the simple style of the gravel path and concrete benches. Photographed 1/08/2008. *Indianapolis Museum of Art Miller House and Garden, Columbus, Indiana, USA. Design: Dan Kiley (garden) with Eero Saarinen (house)*

ABOVE: Gravel path leads through an arched cypress avenue. *Menton, Provence, France. Design: Owner, William Waterfield*

ABOVE: This sandy gravel pathway contrasts with the verdant foliage of the *Betula* (birch) avenue. *The Hidden Gardens, Glasgow, Scotland. Design: nva organisation and City Design Cooperative*

ABOVE RIGHT: Allée of *Carpinus betulus* (hornbeam) box-head trees with gravel, waterfall feature leading to a marble wall with steel abstract sculpture *Big Bite* by Nigel Hall. Tiered hedging in background of *Taxus baccata* (yew). *The Laurent-Perrier Garden, RHS Chelsea Flower Show 2009. Design: Luciano Giubbilei*

RIGHT: *Betula* (birch) avenue with grass pathway leading to an ornamental urn. *Hither Lane, The Hamptons, NY, USA. Design: Reed Hilderbrand*

FAR RIGHT: Pathway leading through avenue of *Malus* (apple) trees underplanted with *Nepeta x faassenii* (catmint). *Cambo Walled Garden, Kingsbarns, Fife, Scotland. Design: Owner, Lady Catherine Erskine and head gardener, Elliot Forsyth*

TOP: Cotswold stone steps are laid into a grass slope and planted with small flowering herbaceous plants in this formal landscaped parkland. *Miserden Park Gardens, Gloucestershire, England. Design: Owner, The Wills family*

ABOVE LEFT: Long, cut stones are inlaid into this lawn punctuating the slope as steps. *Fargo Lane, Irvington, NY, USA. Design: Reed Hilderbrand*

LEFT: A gravel surface leads to contrasting brick paving, stone steps, and is surrounded by a "Cornish hedge". This natural, yet contemporary, style farm garden has an emphasis on sustainabilty and responds to the existing environment. *Tregony, Cornwall, England. Design: David Buurma*

ABOVE: Stone steps leading to the house are inlaid with turf. A rail of metal post and wire, stone walls, slatted wooden screens, and evergreen hedging add a modern aesthetic. *Wellesley, MA, USA. Design: Reed Hilderbrand*

ABOVE: Concrete paving slab steps are softened by campanula and *Alchemilla mollis* (lady's mantle). Metal railings and wooden handrail lead up to the side door of a house. *Stonehaven, Aberdeenshire, Scotland. Design: Owners, Michael and Sue Reid*

ABOVE RIGHT: A tropical garden with patterned stone steps, flanked by planted ceramic urns. Planting includes tropical palms, ferns, and grasses. *Baan Botanica, Bangkok, Thailand. Design: Bensley Design Studios*

RIGHT: This contemporary coastal cottage-style garden has wood-edged steps filled with concrete and inlaid with pebbles and terracotta tiles. *Lip na Cloiche, Ulva Ferry, Isle of Mull, Scotland. Design: Owner, Lucy MacKenzie Panizzon*

FAR LEFT: Cast concrete steps dressed with ceramic pots filled with *Erigeron karvinskianus* (Mexican fleabane). *Ardentinny, Argyllshire, Scotland. Design: Owners, Freda and Barry Waldapfel*

LEFT: Curved cast and rendered concrete steps with ceramic containers containing succulents and coastal plants in a contemporary coastal plantsman's garden. *Bainbridge Island, WA, USA. Design: Owners, Daniel J. Hinkley and Robert Jones*

BELOW LEFT: In this contemporary coastal garden concrete steps inset with lighting are flanked by boulders on one side and a contrasting smooth vertical wall on the other. *Bay Area, San Francisco, CA, USA. Design: Topher Delaney*

RIGHT ABOVE: Coloured and rendered concrete steps tone with natural stone boulders planted with aloes and weigela. *Bainbridge Island, WA, USA. Design: Owners, Daniel J. Hinkley and Robert Jones*

RIGHT: Metal containers of scilla flowers parade up either side of the central section of limestone and gravel steps at The Eden Project. *Bodelva, Cornwall, England. Conceived by Tim Smit. Overall design: Jonathan Ball and Sir Nicholas Grimshaw*

LEFT: Rebar rods shoot up out of the top of a rendered wall with roughcast steps leading through this "gap in the wall" entrance way. Plants include cacti, succulents, and native trees in this contemporary desert garden. *Baja Valley Garden, Paradise Valley, Arizona, USA. Design: Steve Martino*

BELOW: Recycled railway sleeper (railroad tie) steps are planted with herbs and edible plants as ground cover: *Tropaeolum majus* (nasturtium), *Origanum* (oregano), geranium, and *Thymus* (thyme). *Montpelier Cottage, Brilley, Herefordshire, England. Design: Owner, Noel Kingsbury*

ABOVE: Slate steps with a metal edge are surrounded by the contrasting texture of granite chippings in this modernist garden. *Bishopstrow, Warminster, Wiltshire, England. Design: Owner, Michael Newberry*

ABOVE RIGHT: Dressed stone steps with metal handrails are an effective contrast to rough hewn stone walls. *Fargo Lane, Irvington, NY, USA. Design: Reed Hilderbrand*

PAGE RIGHT
RIGHT ABOVE: Stainless steel floating steps, pond, cobbles, and stone paving slabs lead down to a pool with shade-tolerant ferns and aquatic plants in this minimalist modern garden. *Camden, London, England. Design: Dale Loth Architects*

RIGHT: Jetty-style decking with steps lead down to a lawn through large herbaceous perennial borders. *Blackpitts Farm, Towcester, Northamptonshire, England. Design: Owner, James Alexander-Sinclair*

FAR RIGHT: In this minimalist low-maintenance garden ceramic containers are planted with *Chamaerops humilis* and lead the way towards galvanized steps. *Camden, London, England. Design: Owners, Dale Loth Architects*

ABOVE: This pretty gate in Kim Wilde's cottage garden is made from hazel and is embellished with woven heart symbols. It leads your eye by means of a gravel path to a stone urn on a pedestal. *Hertfordshire, England. Design: Owner, Kim Wilde*

LEFT: Automated wooden gates lead into this gravel driveway in a sleek minimalist style. *Hither Lane, The Hamptons, Long Island, NY, USA. Design: Reed Hilderbrand*

FAR LEFT: This bright-red painted wooden gate contrasts vividly with the Scottish landscape. The evergreen hedge of *Ligustrum ovalifolium* (privet) blends and adds a backdrop for the ceramic containers planted with *Leucanthemum vulgare* (oxeye daisy) and red-flowered pelargoniums. *Ardentinny, Argyllshire, Scotland. Design: Freda and Barry Waldapfel*

MIDDLE LEFT: Wooden gates, gravel paths, terracotta containers, and driftwood sculpture all lead the eye through this potager garden to the sea view. *Lip na Cloiche Garden and Nursery, Isle of Mull, Argyllshire, Scotland. Design: Owner, Lucy Mackenzie Panizzon*

LEFT: A simple wooden garden gate at the side of a shed leads out from the garden to fields and flat landscape. *Spalding, Lincolnshire, England. Design: Owners, Freddie Honnor and Maria Stamp*

PAGE RIGHT
TOP LEFT: This Mediterranean-style courtyard garden embraces recycled materials. The focal point of this area is a painted recycled doorway. Even out of season lush climbers flank the garden entrance, a combination of *Hydrangea anomala* subsp. *petiolaris* (climbing hydrangea), variegated *Hedera* (ivy), and *Clematis* 'Bill MacKenzie'. *Edinburgh, Scotland. Design: Owners, Raymond and Gail Paul*

TOP RIGHT: An open rustic wooden gate indicates the way along a brick path to an antique wheelbarrrow and orchard. *Hertfordshire, England. Design: Owner, Kim Wilde*

RIGHT: Oriental-style gateway made of reclaimed wood with antique stone lintel. *San Jose, CA, USA. Design: Owner, Cevan Forristt*

FAR RIGHT: This off-white painted wooden gate with metal bars opens the way to a pretty patterned pebble path though a woodland. The rusting metal rods add a distressed look to the paintwork and echo the lines of moss between the stones. *Summerdale Garden Nursery, Cow Brow, Lupton, Cumbria. Design: Owners, David and Gail Sheals*

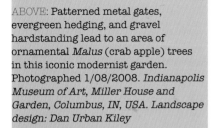

ABOVE: Patterned metal gates, evergreen hedging, and gravel hardstanding lead to an area of ornamental *Malus* (crab apple) trees in this iconic modernist garden. Photographed 1/08/2008. *Indianapolis Museum of Art, Miller House and Garden, Columbus, IN, USA. Landscape design: Dan Urban Kiley*

RIGHT: This wrought-iron gate supported by a brick wall opens to a winter display of cotoneaster berries. *Towcester, Northamptonshire, England. Design: James Alexander-Sinclair*

FAR RIGHT: Rusted steel gates are supported in a wooden frame amidst a lush planting of bamboo in this romantic-style garden. *Portland, OR, USA. Design: Steven J. Maker and Harvey W. Freer*

LEFT: "Soliton Gate" in the wall of the DNA Garden with the "Universe Cascade" in background. The twisted metal gate is studded with two local ammonites and set solidly in the stone wall. *The Garden of Cosmic Speculation, Portrack House, Dumfries and Galloway, Scotland. Design: Charles Jencks and Maggie Keswick*

BELOW: These decorative wrought-iron gates may not open or lead anywhere, but they enhance the view of this cottage-style garden planted with phlox, *Alchemilla mollis* (lady's mantle), hellebores, delphiniums, crocosmia, and fuchsia. *St. Andrews, Fife, Scotland. Design: St. Andrews Preservation Trust*

TOP: This stunning bronze-railed bridge with granite path sweeps in minimalist style. *The Sackler Crossing, The Royal Botanic Gardens Kew, Surrey, England. Design: John Pawson*

ABOVE: A bright red painted Chinese-style bridge showers water on the unsuspecting as they cross in these surprise water gardens. A *Prunus* (flowering cherry) tree brings colour to the foreground. *Chateau de Vendeuvre, France. Design: The Counts of Vendeuvre*

LEFT: A white painted wooden footbridge leads from a meadow planted with crocus and spring bulbs into the woodland of this formal 18th-century garden layout. *House of Pitmuies, Forfar, Angus, Scotland. Design: Owner, Mrs. Farquhar Ogilvie*

ABOVE: Wisteria covers an arched Japanese bridge that crosses the Saxon moat in the grounds of Great Fosters Hotel. *Egham, Surrey, England. Design: W. H. Romaine-Walker and Gilbert Jenkins with recent additions by Kim Wilkie*

ABOVE RIGHT: This dressed-wood and driftwood bridge is surrounded by *Anthriscus sylvestris* (cow parsley) and *Digitalis purpurea* (foxglove) softening the look of this cottage-style coastal garden. *Lip na Cloiche, Ulva Ferry, Isle of Mull, Argyllshire, Scotland. Design: Owner, Lucy Mackenzie Panizzon*

RIGHT: A chunky arching wooden bridge crosses a reconstructed dry riverbed in a garden full of drought-tolerant planting. *The Old Vicarage, East Ruston, Norfolk, England. Design: Owners, Alan Gray and Graham Robeson*

FAR LEFT: A wrought-iron railed and wooden planked footbridge crosses a stream. *Colesbourne Park, Cheltenham, Gloucestershire, England. Design: Owners, the Elwes family*

LEFT: A water-loving *Salix babylonica* (weeping willow) gently drapes its branches over this little curved wooden bridge which provides a walkway over a gushing burn. *Cambo Walled Garden, Fife, Scotland. Restoration design: Owner, Lady Catherine Erskine*

BELOW LEFT: Moss covers this stone bridge with carved text "Artemis FR15" in this iconic artist's romantic garden. *Little Sparta, Dunsyre, Lanarkshire, Scotland. Design: Ian Hamilton-Finlay*

PAGE RIGHT
TOP LEFT: Wooden planked zig-zag boardwalk wends its way through a Japanese garden amongst iris foliage and ferns. *Portland, OR, USA. Design: Professor Takuma Tono*

TOP RIGHT: A raised wooden boardwalk winds and curves with precision over a natural swamp as part of a private environmental project. *West Stockbridge, MA, USA. Design: Reed Hilderbrand*

RIGHT: Cast concrete stepping stones allow access to a woodland garden across a pond of aquatic plants and irises. *Former Heronswood Nursery, Kingston, WA, USA. Design: Owners, Daniel J. Hinkley, and Robert Jones*

FAR RIGHT: Wooden stepping stones lead a path around an abstract lantern structure in a pond designed as a permanent show garden. *"Le jardin des Hesperides", International Garden Festival, Jardin de Metis/Reford Gardens, Quebec, Canada. Design: Andy Cao and Xavier Perrot*

LEFT: An elegant curved pale blue painted wood and metal pergola supports climbing *Rosa* 'Ards Rover', in this exuberant country garden. *Abbey House Gardens, Wiltshire, England. Design: Owners, Ian and Barbara Pollard*

LEFT BELOW: This cut bamboo tunnel allows the light to filter through whilst it links the areas of this oriental-style garden. *La Bambouseraie, Domaine de Prafrance, Anduze, France. Overall design: Eugène Mazel and the Negre family*

ABOVE RIGHT: *Laburnum x watereri* (Golden chain tree) hangs in abundance from this metal arbour with gravel path beneath. *The Queen's Garden, Royal Botanic Gardens Kew, Surrey, England*

ABOVE FAR RIGHT: Climbing roses cover this metal pergola above a brick pathway and long herbaceous perennial borders. *The Madoo Conservancy, Sagaponack, Long Island, NY, USA. Design: Robert Dash*

RIGHT: Pink-flowering *Clematis montana*, *Prunus cerasus* pink blossom, and *Lonicera nitida* all fight for attention on a metal pergola leading to a potager and orchard garden in this suburban garden. *Roscullen, Edinburgh, Scotland. Design: Owner, Mrs. Anne Duncan*

FAR RIGHT: In this contemporary Mediterranean garden *Vitis vinifera* (grape) covers a metal-framed arbour built over wooden-edged raised beds. It leads to a bench at the end of the tunnel. *Le Jardin de L'Alchimiste, Eygalieres en Provence, France. Design: Arnaud Maurières and Eric Ossart*

FAR LEFT: This neat angular pergola supports a trained *Ostrya carpinifolia* (hop hornbeam). Beneath is a steel-edged, gravel and tile path in this contemporary Mediterranean garden. *Le Jardin de L'Alchimiste, Eygalieres en Provence, France. Design: Arnaud Maurières and Eric Ossart*

LEFT: A solid concrete and wood pergola supports climbing wisteria underplanted with *Trachelospermum jasminoides* (star jasmine, confederate jasmine). This Californian garden uses recycled materials wherever possible. *Orinda, CA, USA. Design: Topher Delaney*

LEFT MIDDLE: A woven willow tunnel leads to a wooden framed workshop and office. *The Green Wood Centre, Coalbrookdale, Telford, Shropshire. Design: The Green Wood Trust*

LEFT BOTTOM: Clipped *Carpinus betulus* (hornbeam) archways link arms around this plantsman's garden. *Former Heronswood Nursery, Kingston, WA, USA. Design: Daniel J. Hinkley and Robert Jones*

PAGE RIGHT
TOP LEFT: A wooden pergola with dangling rope supports *Clematis montana* 'Tetrarose' beside the shrub *Griselinia littoralis* in this coastal cottage garden. *Lip na Cloiche, Ulva Ferry, Isle of Mull, Argyllshire, Scotland. Design: Owner, Lucy Mackenzie Panizzon*

TOP RIGHT : Surrounded by large flowering herbaceous perennial borders a *Vitis vinifera* (grape) covers this metal pergola in a walled 19th-century potager garden. *Titsey Place, Oxted, Surrey, England. Design: The Leveson Gower family*

RIGHT: Metal scaffolding poles create a recycled pergola and give a contemporary look to this cottage garden. Planted below for colour are *Papaver* (poppy), *Nigella damascena* (love-in-a-mist), and climbing roses. *Blackpitts Farm, Towcester, Northamptonshire, England. Design: Owner, James Alexander-Sinclair*

FAR RIGHT: *Vitis vinifera* (grape) covers this metal pergola sheltering a terracotta urn and pink-flowering petunias below. *Titsey Place, Oxted, Surrey, England. Design: The Leveson Gower family*

TOP: Herbaceous perennial border of combined silver and purple foliage, including *Cynara scolymus* (globe artichokes), artemisia, heliotrope, and aeoniums, flourishes in The Terrace Garden. *Chanticleer Garden, Wayne, PA, USA. Design: Jonathan Wright*

ABOVE: An infinity swimming pool holds centre stage in this terrace. The stone steps are inlaid with turf; a metal post and wire fence provide the backdrop along with stone walls and slatted wooden screens to the rear. *Wellesley, MA, USA. Design: Reed Hilderbrand*

LEFT: Stone paved patio with plenty of space for relaxing and playing. Wooden benches are built in around the far perimeter. *Salem, NY, USA. Design: Oehme, van Sweden*

TOP RIGHT: Terrace with rendered, dyed concrete paving blends with natural rock outcrops providing a viewing platform to appreciate the sea views and eclectic planting, including aloes, cacti, ornamental grasses, and *Ceanothus* (California lilac). *Windcliff, Bainbridge Island, WA, USA. Design: Daniel J. Hinkley and Robert Jones*

RIGHT: This long Arts & Crafts-style terrace uses stone slab paving and a wooden pergola alongside full herbaceous perennial borders. *Great Fosters Hotel, Egham, Surrey, England. Design: W. H. Romaine-Walker and Gilbert Jenkins, with recent additions by Kim Wilkie*

LEFT TOP: A white painted wooden pergola gateway leads into this patterned brick paved patio. A long water feature and stepping stones feature in this sheltered area of a Mediterranean-style coastal garden. *Santa Barbara, CA, USA. Design: Isabelle Greene*

LEFT: Clean lines of stone paving with flint walls and wood edging make a perfect platform for the wooden outdoor furniture on this contemporary-styled patio. In the foreground a herbaceous perennial border includes *Nepeta racemosa* 'Walker's Low' and *Doronicum* x *excelsum* 'Harpur Crewe'. *"The Savills Garden", RHS Chelsea Flower Show 2007, Design: Marcus Barnett and Philip Nixon*

TOP LEFT: This brick paved patio is a quiet and relaxing area beneath a sloping woodland edged with a natural stone wall. *Salix babylonica* var. *pekinensis* 'Tortuosa' stands in a container in the foreground. *Boston, MA, USA. Design: Owners, Scarlet Bartlett and Adrian Guppy*

ABOVE LEFT: A wooden deck patio with a pergola covered with vine foliage creates a romantic sheltered spot in this country garden. *Shropshire, England. Design: Owner, Jenny Goodrich*

TOP RIGHT: A patio of light gravel overlooks a stone-edged pool, which is fed by a rill. A tree of *Parrotia persica* provides shade and the borders are filled with *Tulipa* 'Orange Emperor', *Fritillaria imperialis*, aloes, and aquilegia (columbine). *The "Foreign & Colonial Investments" Garden, RHS Chelsea Flower Show 2010. Design: Thomas Hoblyn*

ABOVE RIGHT: A formal paved patio decorated with stone and ceramic urns planted with bright red-flowering *Canna* (Indian shot plant) and solenostemon. *The Terrace Garden, Chanticleer Garden, Wayne, PA, USA. Design: Dan Benarcik*

TOP: A woodland garden with a rest area where the stone paving allows ground cover plants to creep between the slabs. Bougainvillea climbs over the wall behind the seating area and pink flowering camellias are in the foreground. *Santa Barbara, CA, USA. Design: Isabelle Greene*

ABOVE: This paved patio area uses soft Mediterranean-style colours to connect the plants with the furnishings, wooden trellis screen, and pergola. Planting includes *Lavandula stoechas* (French lavender), pelargoniums, *Buxus sempervirens*, *Dianthus* (pink), *Erysimum* (wallflower), and *Lilium orientalis* (Oriental lily). *Braid Farm Road, Edinburgh, Scotland. Design: Owners, Raymond and Gail Paul*

ABOVE: A coastal Mediterranean-style garden with grasses and ground cover plants used to accentuate the shapes of the stone paving. *Santa Barbara, CA, USA. Design: Isabelle Greene*

TOP: A restful stone patio sits amid drifts of textured foliage in a "New American Garden" style. Planting includes *Hakonechloa macra* 'Aureola', *Geranium macrorrhizum*, epimedium, astilbe, and bamboo. *The Hamptons, Long Island, NY, USA. Design: Oehme, van Sweden*

ABOVE: This patio uses a combination of herringbone patterned brick and paving stones. The plants in the containers bring colour to the area. *Clibdens, Charlton, Waterlooville, Hampshire, England. Design: Owner, Mrs. J. Budden*

RIGHT: The rambling rose-covered rustic tree-branch pergola creates a romantic setting for an evening glass of wine in this pretty English country garden. *Shropshire, England. Design: Owner, Jenny Goodrich*

LEFT: Dressed stone steps smartly edge this reflecting pool. A slit in the stone wall provides an aperture for water to tumble from and create movement and sound. *Hither Lane, East Hampton, Long Island, NY, USA. Design: Reed Hilderbrand*

BELOW LEFT: This contemporary desert garden uses native plants in the garden to soften the look of the swimming pool set in concrete paving. The tall statuesque cactus is *Carnegiea gigantea* (saguaro). *Paradise Valley, Phoenix, AZ, USA. Design: Steve Martino*

RIGHT: This modernist garden uses wooden decking and brick tiles around the swimming pool in contrast to the smooth rendered walls. Planting includes *Choisya* (Mexican orange blossom), *Rhus*, and bamboo. *Bishopstrow, Wiltshire, England. Design: Michael Newberry*

BELOW: In this new family garden the wooden deck surrounds the swimming pool while hurdle screens and brick walls enclose the leisure area. A converted painted shed has become a convenient changing room. *Spalding, Lincolnshire, England. Design: Owners, Freddie Honnor and Maria Stamp*

LEFT: Stone paving slabs lead to steps below the surface of the swimming pool in this contemporary "New American Style" garden. The drifts of grasses and perennials in the borders are the trademarks. *The Hamptons, Long Island, NY, USA. Design: Oehme, van Sweden*

BELOW LEFT: In the heart of this woodland garden, stone paving surrounds this swimming pool with gentle steps and walls. The concrete rendered columns provide a formal frontage to the pool house. Planting includes *Cyperus papyrus. Santa Barbara, CA, USA. Design: Isabelle Greene*

ABOVE RIGHT: This iconic modernist house and garden sit in the Sonoma Hills. The swimming pool is set in paving and decking, partly framed by *Quercus virginiana* (live oak), some growing through cut-outs in the deck. The garden was the first ever with a designed "kidney"-shaped swimming pool. *The Donnell Garden, Sonoma County, CA, USA. Design: Thomas Church, with Lawrence Halprin and George Rockrise*

RIGHT: Scented lavender around the perimeter with tamarisk and cycads in containers help to create a relaxed atmosphere around this Provençal swimming pool. *Le Mas de la Brune, Eygalieres en Provence, France. Design: Owners, Marie and Alain de Larouzière*

ABOVE: This contemporary desert garden enjoys a swimming pool set in concrete paving surrounded by steel fencing. The shade over the barbecue is made of reinforced metal sheets. *Paradise Valley, Phoenix, AZ, USA. Design: Steve Martino*

RIGHT: A fresh water swimming pond planted with aquatic and marginal plants makes a natural alternative to the normal blue pool. *"A Swimming Pond", Hampton Court Flower Show 2001. Design: Daniel Lloyd-Morgan*

DIVIDE

WALLS
HEDGES
FENCES
SCREENS
TREES
BEDS & BORDERS
RAISED BEDS
SHRUBS
POOLS
FOUNTAINS
SEATING
SCULPTURE
POTS
SUPPORTS
LABELS
HUTS & SHEDS
GREENHOUSES

The first question to ask is why would one want to divide a garden. The reasons can be many: perhaps for privacy, maybe for intrigue. There is also something magical about not being able to see a garden all at once. A tantalising glimpse through a fence or a hedge can alert curiosity and increase interest in a garden space. It can also give the eyes a rest – all the better for taking in the approach to a new area ahead. Whichever way you look at it, to divide need not mean to block out.

The notion of creating garden "rooms" is not new. Some very notable gardens take the form of a series of spaces linked by themes. In around 1910 the American designer Lawrence Johnston started work on the famous Arts and Crafts garden at Hidcote Manor in Gloucestershire, England.

Johnston used yew, holly, and beech hedges to define a series of garden "rooms". One room contains a circular raised pool, while others derive their character from the varied planting designs.

In the 1930s Thomas Church started a landscape architecture practice in San Francisco. He brought with him experiences from foreign travels, particularly in Spain and Italy, and so was able to compare the similarities between the Mediterranean and Californian climates. He often used the idea of the outdoor living space, also dividing the landscape into separate "rooms". In the Sullivan Garden he used a zigzag path to divide a slanted shrub border from the lawn. Later he introduced curved forms, most memorably at the Donnell Garden in Sonoma, California, which was designed on a hilltop around existing mature oaks. The garden, with its iconic kidney-shaped swimming pool echoes the contours of the surrounding hills of the Sonoma Valley below (page 71).

Evergreen hedges are an obvious and reliable way to divide gardens, but there are plenty of other ways to slice the garden into smaller sections. The divider itself can have a purpose. A glasshouse, garden shed, or garage does not need to just house plants, tools, or a car – each structure can become a useful divider as easily as a fence or a hedge.

Clever seating can also make a difference to how a garden is viewed. Where you sit can divide what you see from what you don't. What's behind you becomes invisible – unless of course there is reflection. Mirrors can camouflage divisions, making them seemingly transparent or they can provide an impression of infinity. A view can be diffused when viewed through a fountain, while a river or stream can separate a landscape like a ribbon on a parcel. Running water can also provide sound to distract the mind.

Levels too are an important provider of division. The M25 motorway is one of the busiest and most congested roads in the United Kingdom. Near it is Great Fosters, a building of historic importance that is surrounded by 50 acres of formal gardens and parkland. Despite its proximity to the busy road it remains out of view and tranquil. Here contemporary landscape architect Kim Wilkie ingeniously provided protection from the intrusion of the noise and sight of the motorway with 20-foot high earthworks in the form of a turf amphitheatre (page 245).

Dividing gardens can also increase the impression of scale. One of my favourite small country gardens, Ivan and Sadie Hall's cottage garden (page 151), is about a quarter of an acre in total size. Because it is divided so successfully into contrasting styles and themes it gives the impression of being far larger than it actually is.

On a larger scale, Parc André Citroën in Paris (page 115) cleverly achieves the same effect in reverse. The 35-acre park is broken down into themed areas and utilizes a number of features illustrated in this chapter, including greenhouses, pools, and raised beds. The six serial gardens are each associated with a metal, a planet, a day of the week, a state of water, and a sense. The overall effect is to divide the area into accessible "bite size" spaces which can then be enjoyed on a more intimate level.

In fact, there is a fine line between dividing and connecting. Clever use of plants (supported or freestanding), walls, fences, screens, water, and levels can all contribute to separating areas of garden space and in so doing add texture, style, and most importantly, intrigue.

RIGHT: Indianapolis Museum of Art Miller House and Garden, Columbus, IN, USA. Photographed: 1/08/2008. Design: Dan Kiley

TOP: This contemporary garden uses a chunky wooden fence that combines as a raised bed. Climbing plants include *Clematis armandii*, while in the bed there is a *Dicksonia antarctica* (Tasmanian tree fern), and in the containers a combination of herbs and flowers: rosemary, sage, oregano, and *Calibrachoa* 'Million Bells'. *Islington, London, England. Design: Joe Swift and The Plantroom*

ABOVE LEFT: This long purple-coloured retaining wall acts as a border between a native Californian meadow planting and drifts of *Stipa tenuissima* (Mexican feather grass) and perennials. *Napa Valley, CA, USA. Design: Topher Delaney*

ABOVE RIGHT: Stone retaining walls enhance the slope of a grass lawn. *Fargo Lane, Irvington, NY, USA. Design: Reed Hilderbrand*

PAGE RIGHT
CLOCKWISE FROM TOP LEFT:
The coloured surface of this retaining wall contrasts with the soft foliage of *Stipa tenuissima* (Mexican feather grass). *Napa Valley, CA, USA. Design: Topher Delaney*

Drystone wall built with local stone overhung by *Olearia macrodonta* (daisy bush) and *Digitalis purpurea* (foxglove). *Lip na Cloiche, Ulva Ferry, Isle of Mull, Argyllshire, Scotland. Design: Owner, Lucy Mackenzie Panizzon*

Gabion wall filled with logs in small modern front garden. *"Reclaim your Garden" by SAC Ayr, Gardening Scotland 2010. Design: Carol Shaw*

Recycled roughcast concrete slabs are used as a retaining wall and interplanted with *Kniphofia* (red hot poker), ornamental grass, and *Tamarix* (tamarisk). *Orinda, CA, USA. Design: Topher Delaney*

Ceramic bamboo sculptures with disporum foliage against claret-coloured wood shingle wall. *Bainbridge*

Island, WA, USA. Design: Owners, Daniel J. Hinkley and Robert Jones. Ceramic bamboo design: Marcia Donahue

Tropical raised pond made from coral and cement filled with *Eichhornia crassipes* (water hyacinth). Barbados. Design: Owner, Kevin Talma

PAGE LEFT
ABOVE LEFT: Brick barn walls and buttresses with Ilex (holly). *Nursted Barns, Petersfield, Hampshire, England. Design: Acres Wild*

ABOVE RIGHT: Natural-style farm garden with emphasis on sustainabilty with stone walls. The climbing plants include a trained espalier Pyrus (pear) tree and climbing rose in flower. *Tregony, Cornwall, England. Design: David Buurma*

LEFT: Rendered concrete walls, steel mesh screens and sheets in a contemporary garden designed to display art alongside Mediterranean planting. The planting includes Trachelospermum jasminoides (star jasmine) and Tulbaghia violacea (society garlic, pink agapanthus). *Orinda, CA, USA. Design: Topher Delaney*

TOP LEFT: Flint and brick walls with gravel hardstanding create a cottage garden style with Laurus nobilis (bay), agave, and helichrysum. *Clibdens, Waterlooville, Hampshire, England. Design: Mrs. J. Budden*

TOP MIDDLE: Stone wall, climbing rose, Lavandula (lavender), and Verbena bonariensis. *Tregony, Cornwall, England. Design: David Buurma*

TOP RIGHT: Red brick wall with zinc and terracotta containers. The planting includes Ipomoea (morning glory), wisteria climber, and dahlia. *Blackpitts Farm, Towcester, Northamptonshire, England. Design: James Alexander-Sinclair*

ABOVE: Wisteria sinensis 'Alba' climbing a plastered wall. *Chapel, Palheiro Gardens, Madeira, Portugal. Design: The Blandy family*

THIS PAGE CLOCKWISE:
> Slates
> Stone and cement wall
> Cornish drystone wall with turf
> Metal gabion filled with bricks
> Recycled brick wall

THIS PAGE CLOCKWISE:
> Cornish drystone wall with turf
> Rendered concrete with inlaid glass marbles
> Wire gabion and rock
> Pennsylvania flagstone (bluestone)
> Weathered wood cladding

ABOVE: A range of evergreen plants are used to create a forest of topiary shapes. *Remsenburg, Long Island, NY, USA. Design: Owners, Jack Waxman and Bernard J. Dubin*

LEFT: Snow helps to define the year-round interest of *Taxus baccata* (yew) topiary and hedges. *Towcester, Sholebroke Lodge, Northamptonshire, England. Design: Owner, Deirdre Fenwick*

BELOW: A display of topiary shapes using *Buxus microphylla x antzam antarctica* (Littleleaf boxwood). *Enid Haupt Conservatory, New York Botanical Garden, NY, USA*

ABOVE: *Buxus sempervirens* parterre and topiary spirals act as a green foil to the terracotta of containers and the brick walled garden. *Lancaster, Lancashire, England. Design: David Redmore*

ABOVE RIGHT: This abstract-shaped *Taxus baccata* (yew) topiary sits over a bed of *Alchemilla mollis* (lady's mantle). *Great Fosters Hotel, Surrey, England. Design: Kim Wilkie*

RIGHT: Clipped *Fagus sylvatica* (beech) trees are used to make strong vertical columns in a lawn. *Blackpitts Farm, Northamptonshire, England. Design: James Alexander-Sinclair*

LEFT: A long narrow avenue of clipped *Taxus baccata* (yew) hedges and lawn creates a sense of distance. *Miserden Park, Gloucestershire, England. Design: Owners, the Wills family*

LEFT BELOW: In this modernist garden an off-set row of *Thuja occidentalis* hedges give necessary privacy and depth without creating a blank wall. Photographed 1/08/2008. *Indianapolis Museum of Art, Miller House and Garden, Columbus, IN, USA. Design: Dan Urban Kiley*

RIGHT: This curved planting of *Carpinus betulus* (hornbeam) trees gives an unusual focus to the enclosed perennials. *Marchants Hardy Plants, East Sussex, England. Design: Owners, Graham Gough and Lucy Goffin*

BELOW: A shaped *Carpinus betulus* (hornbeam) hedge creates enough depth for a *Prunus* (ornamental cherry) to sit back within it. Alliums, irises, and tulips are amongst the planting in the foreground. *Sweden. Design: Owners, Eva and Roland Gustavsson*

ABOVE LEFT: Staggered undulating *Crataegus* (hawthorn) hedges show that hedges need not be just straight lines. *Marchants Hardy Plants, East Sussex, England. Design: Owners, Graham Gough and Lucy Goffin*

ABOVE: Rows of this evergreen *Thuja occidentalis* hedge give protection to a river of shade-loving ground cover plants. Photographed 1/08/2008. *Indianapolis Museum of Art, Miller House and Garden, Columbus, IN, USA. Design: Dan Urban Kiley*

LEFT: *Taxus baccata* (yew) hedges planted in undulating lines help break up the symmetry of a large lawn. *Great Fosters Hotel, Surrey, England. Design: W. H. Romaine-Walker and Gilbert Jenkins with renovations by Kim Wilkie*

RIGHT: Curving *Buxus sempervirens* hedges create strong structure and evergreen colour in this ancient Moorish courtyard. *The High Gardens, Generalife, Alhambra, Spain*

RIGHT BELOW: Combining evergreen variegated euonymus and *Buxus sempervirens* hedging plants successfully creates year-round interest, form, and colour. *Bourne, Lincolnshire, England. Design: Owners, Ivan and Sadie Hall*

LEFT: In this public garden *Salix* (willow) is woven into a living fence. *Diana, Princess of Wales Memorial Playground, Kensington Gardens, London, England. Fence design: Jim Buchanan*

LEFT BELOW: This Danish garden uses interwoven poplar trees as a living fence, an alternative to normal wooden fencing panels. *Denmark. Design: Owner, Jane Schul*

RIGHT: *Salix* (willow) saplings create a criss-cross pattern for a rustic country cottage effect. *Marchants Hardy Plants, East Sussex, England. Design: Owners, Graham Gough and Lucy Goffin*

PAGE LEFT

FAR LEFT: Cut hazel branches are interwoven here to create a fence structure. Roses and *Prunus spinosa* (blackthorn) are used as additional planting to soften with flower and foliage. *Marchants Hardy Plants, East Sussex, England. Design: Owners, Graham Gough and Lucy Goffin*

LEFT: In this country garden hazel branches are woven to create a barrier then interplanted with traditional hedging plants including *Crataegus* (hawthorn) and *Prunus spinosa* (blackthorn). *Marchants Hardy Plants, East Sussex, England. Design: Owners, Graham Gough and Lucy Goffin*

BELOW: Sculptural structures of woven *Salix* (willow) have been grown here to form a tunnel. Ground cover of *Myosotis* (forget-me-not) flowers. *The Green Wood Centre, Shropshire, England. Design: The Green Wood Trust*

THIS PAGE

LEFT AND BELOW: Fences need not just be straight. This nursery uses sticks of different lengths to create undulations while allowing for views through to other green spaces. *Marchants Hardy Plants, East Sussex, England. Design: Owners, Graham Gough and Lucy Goffin*

FAR LEFT AND LEFT: These driftwood post fences make an artistic and inexpensive alternative to conventional fencing. *Lip na Cloiche Garden and Nursery, Ulva Ferry, Isle of Mull, Argyllshire, Scotland. Design: Owner, Lucy Mackenzie Panizzon*

BELOW LEFT: Wicker hurdle fence screens provide privacy and give a country cottage-style backdrop to flowering plum trees. *Lancaster, Lancashire, England. Design: David Redmore*

BELOW RIGHT: A simple wooden post fence and bench seat create a modest barrier at the end of this grass garden path amongst *Salix* (willow) trees. *Narcissus* (daffodil) have been allowed to naturalize in the lawn. *Marchants Hardy Plants, East Sussex, England. Design: Owners, Graham Gough and Lucy Goffin*

ABOVE: Two contrasting barrier techniques are illustrated here in one place. A woven wicker screen fence in the foreground and an evergreen boxwood hedge at a right angle behind. *Marchants Hardy Plants, East Sussex, England. Design: Owners, Graham Gough and Lucy Goffin*

BELOW: This stainless steel post fence snakes around the pool area to act as a safety fence without blocking views in this Long Island garden. *Hither Lane, The Hamptons, NY, USA. Design: Reed Hilderbrand*

LEFT: A washing line of fabric curtains gives a light and delicate contrast to the dark evergreen of a cypress hedge providing an unusual way of dividing the garden. *Le Jardin de l'Alchimiste, Eygalieres en Provence, France. Design: Arnaud Maurières & Éric Ossart*

LEFT BELOW: Living *Salix* (willow) woven screens encase beds of Mediterranean herbal plants such as *Olea europaea* (olive) trees and *Lavandula* (lavender). *Le Jardin de l'Alchimiste, Eygalieres en Provence, France. Design: Arnaud Maurières & Éric Ossart*

ABOVE: These smart minimal wooden screens act as a windbreak and allow a restricted view to other areas of the garden giving a degree of privacy to this swimming pool terrace. *Wellesley, MA, USA. Design: Reed Hilderbrand*

BELOW: Densely planted hardy bamboos show how successful they can be as screening plants. *La Bambouseraie, Domaine de Prafrance, France. Design: Owners, Eugène Mazel and the Negre family*

LEFT: This woven bamboo makes a lightweight but durable screen. *La Bambouseraie, Domaine de Prafrance, Anduze, France. Design: Owners, the Negre family*

ABOVE: These wooden posts have been painted in tones of green to make a striking, but sympathetic, screen dividing the gravel path from a woodland area in this public garden venue. *International Garden Festival, Jardin de Metis/Reford Gardens, Quebec, Canada*

RIGHT: Recycled old window frames are used here as a screen device amongst a large perennial grass border. *Landenberg, PA, USA. Design: Owners, Rick Darke and Melinda Zoehrer*

BELOW LEFT: Metal clad screen contrasts well with the delicacy of perennial plants *Panicum virgatum, Lindera benzoin,* and *Halesia diptera. Landenberg, PA, USA. Design: Owners, Rick Darke and Melinda Zoehrer*

BELOW MIDDLE: This woven sheet of aluminium and recycled rebar rods makes a clean-looking contemporary screen for this desert garden. *Baja Canyon Garden, Paradise Valley, Phoenix, AZ, USA. Design: Steve Martino*

BELOW RIGHT: Industrial metal post and mesh screens are used here to support climbing plants. *Phoenix Museum of Modern Art, AZ, USA. Design: Reed Hilderbrand*

PAGE RIGHT

LEFT: Poplar trees have been shaped to create sculptural forms in this iconic Swedish garden. *Södra Sandby, Sweden. Design: Owner, Sven Ingvar Andersson*

BELOW: This overturned and cleaned tree stump has been used as a garden feature with campanula used as ground cover. *Waterlooville, Hampshire, England. Design: Owner, Mrs. J. Budden*

FAR RIGHT: This modernist garden uses *Malus* (crab apple) trees between concrete slabs and *Impatiens walleriana* (busy lizzie) with *Hedera* (ivy) ground cover to create a checkerboard grid pattern. Photographed 1/08/2008. *Indianapolis Museum of Art, Miller House and Garden, Columbus, IN, USA. Design: Daniel Urban Kiley*

BELOW LEFT: This contemporary garden installation uses translucent tubes of "core samples" (materials) to blend with trees between mounds of planted perennial cereal grasses, including rye, barley, oats, and triticale. *"Core Sample", International Garden Festival, Jardin de Metis/Reford Gardens, Quebec, Canada. Design: Pete and Alissa North*

BOTTOM LEFT: Uplighters enhance the driveway planted with *Betula utilis* 'Jacquemontii' (Himalayan birch), and underplanted with *Helleborus* (hellebore) and *Anemone nemerosa*. *Lancaster, Lancashire, England. Design: David Redmore*

BELOW RIGHT: Poplar trees in this installation garden, "soundFIELD", hide sound speakers powered by small wind turbines. *International Garden Festival, Jardin de Metis/Reford Gardens, Quebec, Canada. Design: Douglas Moffat and Steve Bates*

BOTTOM RIGHT: A contemporary display of birch trees, coiled rope, and steel petanque balls enclosed by a metal mesh screen wall with barcode design. *"Garden Play", Cornerstone Sonoma Festival of Gardens, Sonoma, CA, USA. Design: Topher Delaney*

101

TOP LEFT: Tightly clipped and shaped *Pinus sylvestris* 'Watereri' grows through a soft carpet of *Festuca gautieri* framed by granite blocks and *Campanula rotundifolia*. *"The Daily Telegraph Garden"*, *RHS Chelsea Flower Show 2009. Design: Ulf Nordfjell*

MIDDLE: A solitary *Morus nigra* (black mulberry) planted as a specimen tree in the gravel area of this garden. *Hertfordshire, England. Design: Owner, Kim Wilde*

ABOVE: Evergreen planting of a pittosporum hedge contrasts with a standard clipped *Elaeagnus* x *ebbingei*. *Eden Project, Cornwall, England. Landscape Design: Land Use Consultants*

LEFT: Two silver-leaved *Pyrus salicifolia* 'Pendula' (weeping pear) grow through squares of clipped *Buxus sempervirens* hedging. *Waterlooville, Hampshire, England. Design: Owner, Mrs. J. Budden*

RIGHT: This sunny courtyard garden features a row of rowan trees amongst the stone paving. *Tregony, Cornwall, England. Design: David Buurma*

BELOW LEFT: Orange trees sweep through ancient Moorish courtyard gardens between tracks of *Buxus sempervirens* hedging. *The Alhambra, Granada, Spain*

BELOW MIDDLE: This small, square island bed placed in gravel with steel edging contains *Acer griseum* (paperbark maple). The uplighter enhances its glowing translucent bark. *Orinda, CA, USA. Design: Topher Delaney*

BELOW RIGHT: A terracotta pot containing a silver-leaved *Eucalyptus* (gum) tree stands proud amongst containers of herbs and a fire pit on the deck in this town garden. *Twickenham, London, England. Design: Owner, Ian Sidaway*

LEFT: Water around these *Olea europaea* (olive) trees and *Bellis perennis* (daisy) on paved platform beds creates an island effect. *"A Garden for All Time"*, *Evening Standard Garden, RHS Chelsea Flower Show 2000. Design: Arabella Lennox-Boyd*

BELOW LEFT: *Crataegus* (hawthorn) trees here are trained into a tall pergola-like hedge. *Marchants Hardy Plants, Laughton, East Sussex, England. Design: Graham Gough and Lucy Goffin*

BELOW RIGHT: A layer of fresh snow covering this small *Prunus* (ornamental cherry) tree accentuates its form. *Towcester, Northamptonshire, England. Design: James Alexander-Sinclair*

BOTTOM LEFT: An uplighter highlights the shape of a *Quercus virginiana* (southern live oak) in this coastal garden with terraced lawns and large border of ornamental grasses. *Bay Area, San Francisco, CA, USA. Design: Topher Delaney*

BOTTOM RIGHT: A favourite old *Malus* (apple) tree in blossom leans on its prop in this historic orchard garden. *Skagit Valley, WA, USA. Design: Dick and Lavone Reim*

ABOVE: Gabions edged with reclaimed bricks are used as a raised bed for planting *Betula* (birch) trees. *The Hidden Gardens, Glasgow, Scotland. Design: nva organisation and City Design Cooperative*

ABOVE RIGHT: Two columns of evergreen *Taxus baccata* 'Fastigiata Aureomarginata' (golden Irish yew) mark the entrance to a garden path.

Colourful *Geranium psilostemon* and *Lavandula* (lavender) add flowering colour. *Hampshire, England. Design: Owner, Mrs. J. Budden*

RIGHT: A wooden pavilion built around the trunk of a *Quercus robur* (English oak) tree emphasizes height, shape, and texture. *The Hidden Gardens, Glasgow, Scotland. Design: nva organisation and City Design Cooperative*

LEFT: Long border with uniform lines of plants, including heuchera, lavender, ornamental grasses, and herbs, helps to emphasize the approach to the garden entrance. *Jardin Lineaire, Les Jardins de Metis and Reford Historic Gardens, Quebec, Canada. Design: Vlan Paysages*

BELOW: Striking spring colour is created here by this mass planting of bulbs: *Tulipa* 'Red Impression' (outer), *Tulipa* 'Princess Charmante' (middle), *Tulipa* 'Sevilla' (inner), and a centre bed of blue muscari. *Floriade, Holland, 2002. Design: Jacqueline van der Kloet*

PREVIOUS PAGES
LEFT TOP: Densely planted flowering herbaceous borders reflected in long ponds. *Carnell Estates, Hurlford, Ayrshire, Scotland. Design: Owners, the Findlay family*

LEFT BOTTOM: Victorian walled garden with herbaceous perennial borders and trained fruit trees. Significant plants include *Onopordum acanthium* (Scotch thistle), *Eremurus* (Foxtail lily), and *Crambe cordifola. Cambo Walled Garden, Kingsbarns, Fife, Scotland. Design: Owner, Lady Catherine Erskine and head gardener, Elliot Forsyth*

RIGHT TOP: Herbaceous perennial border with repeat planting of *Filipendula* (meadowsweet), dahlia, *Foeniculum vulgare* (fennel), and *Scabiosa* (scabious) with anchor plants of *Acer griseum* and scefflera. *The Dillon Garden, Dublin, Ireland. Design: Owner, Helen Dillon*

RIGHT MIDDLE: Soft and delicate plants contrast against the solidity of *Taxus baccata* (yew) hedging. Ornamental grass *Molinia caerulea* subsp. *arundinacea* 'Transparent', helenium, echinops, eryngium, astilbe, and *Actaea* 'James Compton' feature. *Hummelo, Holland. Design: Owner, Piet Oudolf*

RIGHT BOTTOM: This enclosed courtyard garden is filled with an eclectic mix of plants focussing on foliage with texture and a yellow, green, and gold theme. Plants include *Millium effusum* 'Aureum' (Bowles' golden grass), carex, iris, bergenia, and *Cordyline* (cabbage palm). *The former Heronswood Nursery, Bainbridge Island, WA, USA. Design: Owners, Daniel J. Hinkley and Robert Jones*

RIGHT: A curved spring border echoes the natural lines of this suburban garden allowing an intimate pathway to a woodland area. Plants include many varieties of narcissus plus *heuchera*, scilla, muscari, tiarella, iris, and euphorbia. *Lancaster, Lancashire, England. Design: David Redmore*

BELOW LEFT: This narrow border between concrete paving and a retaining wall is an ideal space for drought-tolerant *Sempervivum* (houseleek) and *Achillea* (yarrow) to flourish in the Californian sun. *Napa, CA, USA. Design: Topher Delaney*

BELOW RIGHT: Borders containing a mass of perennial plants soften the look of this narrow path. Red-leaved canna, sanguisorba, dahlia, and filipendula lead towards an *Acer griseum* (paperbark maple). *The Dillon Garden, Dublin, Ireland. Design: Owner, Helen Dillon*

LEFT: White-flowering *Daphne caucasica* feature in these oval-shaped shrub borders beneath ornamental cherry trees. *Cambridge, MA, USA. Design: Reed Hilderbrand*

BELOW LEFT: This small bed of annual busy lizzies brings a highlight of colour. Photographed 1/08/2008. *Indianapolis Museum of Art Miller House and Garden, Columbus, IN, USA. Design: Dan Urban Kiley*

BELOW RIGHT: A collection of *Iris sibirica* varieties add texture and colour to this landscaped woodland garden. *Irvington, NY, USA. Design: Reed Hilderbrand.*

BOTTOM: This undulating border design uses plants with dark purple foliage, including *Acer palmatum* 'Atropurpureum', *Ophiopogon nigrescens*, *Physocarpus* (ninebark), and *Phormium* (New Zealand flax). Highlights are added by *Rosa* 'Princess of Wales' and *Heuchera* 'Pewter Moon'. *The Salvation Army Garden, RHS Chelsea Flower Show 2004. Design: Julian Dowle*

RIGHT: Borders of spring bulbs including tulips, hyacinths, *Fritillaria imperialis* (crown imperial), daffodils, and grape hyacinth put together to make a vivid statement. *Keukenhof, Lisse, Holland. Design: Jacqueline van der Kloet*

FAR RIGHT: A long border of herbaceous perennials is given scale and protection by a shelter belt of poplar trees. *The Madoo Conservancy, Long Island, NY, USA. Design: Owner, Robert Dash*

ABOVE: Against the Corten steel
backdrop *Viburnum rhytidophyllum*
stands proud. *Stipa gigantea*
punctuates this purple and blue border
achieved by mixing plants such as Iris
'Attention Please', *Allium hollandicum*
'Purple Sensation', *Astrantia major*
'Claret', and *Nepeta racemosa* 'Walker's
Low'. *Buxus sempervirens* hedge
provides texture in the foreground.
"The Daily Telegraph Garden", RHS
*Chelsea Flower Show 2006, London,
England. Design: Tom Stuart-Smith*

LEFT ABOVE: An old tin bathtub makes an interesting raised bed for tiny alpine and succulent plants. *Lip na Cloiche Garden & Nursery, Ulva Ferry, Isle of Mull, Argyllshire, Scotland. Design: Owner, Lucy Mackenzie Panizzon*

LEFT: Zinc water tanks built into a flint wall provide raised beds for a selection of hostas. *Hampshire, England. Design: Owner, Mrs. J. Budden*

ABOVE: Recycled roughcast concrete slabs make a raised trough for *Asparagus densiflorus* (asparagus fern), *Sempervivum* (houseleek), *Euphorbia rigida*, and pelargoniums. *Orinda, CA, USA. Design: Topher Delaney*

RIGHT: Staggered raised beds create a theatre of textured sedums and perennials crowned with a mass of mauve-flowering *Perovskia* (Russian sage). *Parc André Citroën, Paris, France. Design: Gilles Clément, Patrick Berger, Alain Provost, Jean-Paul Viguier, Jean-François Jodry*

ABOVE: This city courtyard garden uses tiles to create a smart framework for the raised beds and pond. Plants include *Zantedeschia aethiopica* (calla lily), *Acer palmatum* (Japanese maple), heuchera, bamboo, and Alliums. *Hackney, London, England. Design: Joe Swift*

RIGHT ABOVE: Metal gabion cages filled with stones provide strong walls for these raised beds. Lavender, comfrey, and sage are amongst the herbs grown at a height here for visitors to enjoy the scent. *The Hidden Gardens, Glasgow, Scotland. Design: nva organisation and City Design Cooperative*

RIGHT: A stone retaining wall doubles here as a raised border enclosing contrasting textures of soft feminine roses and cotoneaster shrubs. *Irvington, NY, USA. Design: Reed Hilderbrand*

LEFT: Cast concrete inset with glass beads is used here to create curving raised bed walls in this cafe garden. Herbal and edible plants including *Laurus nobilis* (bay) and *Humulus lupulus* 'Aurea' (golden hop) fill the beds. *WXD Cafe, Crouch End, London. Design: Steve Bradley and Dan Pearson*

BELOW: The length of these raised beds is accentuated by repeat planting of *Perovskia* (Russian sage), lavender, and *Alchemilla mollis* (lady's mantle). *Boston, MA, USA. Design: Reed Hilderbrand*

BOTTOM: Brick edges create the centre raised bed here but it is surrounded by further beds of *Buxus sempervirens* in this colourful garden. Outer borders are filled with a collection of hemerocallis and kniphofia. *Apple Court, Hampshire, England. Design: Roger Grounds and Diana Grenfell*

BELOW: Wooden posts are used here as a neat edge to the border where purple-flowering *Verbena bonariensis* is flourishing. *Hertfordshire, England. Design: James Alexander-Sinclair*

FAR RIGHT TOP: Here lengths of interlocking planks are used to make a compact raised cutting garden for plants including *Salvia mexicana* 'Limelight' (Mexican sage) and helenium. *Napa, CA, USA.*

FAR RIGHT BOTTOM: A curving wall of bricks is enough to raise this border up from the surrounding gravel hardstanding. The feathery plants include echinops, macleaya, euphorbia, *Centranthus ruber*, stachys, heuchera, *Cynara cardunculus* (cardoon), acanthus, and *Foeniculum vulgare* (fennel). *Hertfordshire, England. Design: Owner, Kim Wilde*

ABOVE: Hydrangeas and hostas are reflected in this small pond creating a pretty garden of pastel colours. Shrubs include *Hydrangea macrophylla* 'Souvenir de Mme. E. Chautard' and *H. macrophylla* 'La Marne'. *Belgian Hydrangea Society collection and display garden, Destelbergen, Ghent, Belgium*

RIGHT TOP: Evergreen hebe provides structure and solidity to the soft drifts of achillea, echinacea, and the ornamental grass *Carex. Hampshire, England. Design: Acres Wild*

RIGHT: The easy to grow flowering shrub spiraea provides a pretty foreground to this elegant woodland garden. *Irvington, NY, USA. Design: Reed Hilderbrand*

FAR RIGHT: This deciduous shrub *Salix exigua* (Coyote willow) forms a delicate backdrop for a border of *Stipa arundinacea, Allium* 'Purple Sensation', and *Anthriscus sylvestris. Towcester, Northamptonshire, England. Design: Owner, James Alexander-Sinclair*

LEFT: The sculptural stems of *Viburnum rhytidophyllum* rise and twist out of the low green foliage of *Buxus sempervirens* contrasting with the solidity of the corten steel wall behind. *"The Telegraph Garden"*, *RHS Chelsea Flower Show 2006. Design: Tom Stuart-Smith*

ABOVE: *Cornus alba Sibirica* (red-barked dogwood) and yucca give colour and stature in this winter garden. *Wakehurst Place, West Sussex, England.*

ABOVE RIGHT: Columns of evergreen *Taxus baccata* (yew) stand erect amongst snow-covered shrubs, ornamental grasses, and seedheads of herbaceous perennials. *Blackpitts Farm, Towcester, Northamptonshire, England. Design: Owner, James Alexander-Sinclair*

RIGHT: *Berberis thunbergii Atropurpurea* and *Berberis darwinii* combine to make an interesting colour combination. *Moors Meadow, Bromyard, Herefordshire, England Design: Owner, Ros Bissell*

FAR RIGHT: A shaggy mane of yellow flowering broom (genista or cytisus) flops over a contrasting blue painted bench. *Denmans Garden, Sussex, England. Design: Owner, John Brookes*

ABOVE: Carefully placed shrubs, *Rosa glauca*, *Buxus sempervirens*, *Lonicera nitida*, and the deciduous *Rhus typhina* give structure to the gentleness of these cottage garden herbaceous borders. *Ardentinny, Argyllshire, Scotland. Design: Owners, Barry and Freda Waldapfel*

ABOVE RIGHT: Pom-poms of white flowering *Viburnum carlesii* make a pretty contrast with the long straight flower-covered branches of *Cercis reniformis* (western redbud). *Chanticleer Garden, Wayne, PA, USA. Design: Chris Woods*

FAR LEFT: A terrace of pools amongst the boulders creates a cool feature in this coastal plantsman's garden. In the distance are *Arbutus menziesii* (Pacific madrone) trees. *Windcliff, Bainbridge Island, WA, USA. Design: Owners, Daniel J. Hinkley and Robert Jones*

LEFT: A square reflecting pool is the focal point of this enclosed courtyard with dark gravel and slate surface planted with *Ostrya carpinifolia* (European hop hornbeam). *"The Black Work" garden, Le Jardin de l'Alchimiste, Eygalieres en Provence, France. Design: Arnaud Maurières and Éric Ossart*

LEFT BELOW: The centrepiece of this contemporary garden is the raised pond made of concrete and surrounded by herbaceous borders. Plants include zantedeschia, libertia, banana, thalictrum, iris, magnolia, *Sciadopitys* (Japanese umbrella pine), peony, and fruit trees. *Portland, OR, USA. Design: Owners, Norm Kalbfleisch and Neil Matteucci*

ABOVE RIGHT: In this contemporary walled parterre garden the reflecting pools create a sense of calm. The all-weather wicker seating is positioned regally on the stone paving. Surrounding plants include *Leucojum aestivum* (summer snowflake), *Magnolia stellata*, *Buxus sempervirens*, climbing roses, and viburnum. *Lancaster, Lancashire, England. Design: David Redmore*

RIGHT BELOW: This square marble fountain overspills into a second pond surrounded by beds of ornamental grasses including *Stipa gigantea*. *Bonython Estate Gardens, Helston, Cornwall, England. Design: Owner, Sue Nathan*

RIGHT: A beautiful Irish town garden featuring a circular concrete pool with fountain and rill set in cobble stones. Metal pergolas in the background support a variegated ivy. *The Dillon Garden, Dublin, Ireland. Design: Owner, Helen Dillon*

BELOW: City basement garden with a ceramic trough water feature framed by antique Moroccan wooden doors, bamboo foliage, and hardy ferns. *Paddington, London, England. Design: James Alexander-Sinclair*

BELOW RIGHT: This contemporary city garden uses tiles to frame the pool and metal containers to hold the *Zantedeschia aethiopica* (calla lily). *Hackney, London, England. Design: Joe Swift and The Plant Room*

LEFT: Large concrete sculptural vessel by French artists Serge and Agnes Bottagisio-Decoux, on stone plinth. *"The Saga Insurance Garden", RHS Chelsea Flower Show 2006. Design: Cleve West*

BELOW LEFT: Over the edge of this pool hangs *Leucojum aestivum* (summer snowflake). The corner bed is planted with *Magnolia stellata*, daphne, and *Helleborus foetidus. Lancaster, Lancashire, England. Design: David Redmore*

LEFT TOP: This conservatory with indoor pool reflects a vast collection of house plants. *Lancaster, Lancashire, England. Design: David Redmore*

LEFT BELOW: Ferns nestle in the slate chipping mulch around the base of slate fountains in this contemporary city garden. *Hackney, London, England. Design: Joe Swift and The Plant Room*

TOP: Magnificent community waterfall and fountain made from concrete and planted with pine trees and rhododendrons. *Keller Fountain Park, Portland, OR, USA. Design: Angela Danadjieva at Lawrence Halprin*

ABOVE LEFT: Edged with rusted steel this shallow canal-style water feature extends through a stone wall into the courtyard of a country garden. *Tregony, Cornwall. Design: David Buurma*

LEFT: Rusted Corten steel is used to create a combined raised bed (filled with *Buxus sempervirens*) and water feature. Oak is used for the decking and bench. *"The Daily Telegraph Garden", RHS Chelsea Flower Show 2006. Design: Tom Stuart-Smith*

ABOVE: Waterfalls cascade down the stone walls of this pond with mysterious sunken marble heads. *Chanticleer Garden, PA, USA. Design: Chris Woods and Mara Baird. Sculpture design: Marcia Donahue*

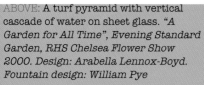
ABOVE: A turf pyramid with vertical cascade of water on sheet glass. *"A Garden for All Time"*, *Evening Standard Garden, RHS Chelsea Flower Show 2000. Design: Arabella Lennox-Boyd. Fountain design: William Pye*

ABOVE RIGHT: Amongst squares of *Buxus sempervirens* surrounded by cloud-pruned hedging a jet of water leaps from one concave stainless steel receptacle to the next. *"Evolution", The Gardens Illustrated Garden, RHS Chelsea Flower Show 2000. Design: Arne Maynard and Piet Oudolf*

RIGHT: Multiple fountains play in the pools in this ancient Moorish courtyard garden. *The Soultana's Court, The Alhambra, Spain*

ABOVE: The fountain in this circular pond is surrounded by large drifts of ornamental grasses and flowering perennial plants. *The Walled Garden, Scampston, Yorkshire, England. Planting design: Piet Oudolf*

FAR LEFT: This metal fountain in a circular stone pool juxtaposes with the checkerboard grid of *Malus* (crab apple) trees. Photographed 1/08/2008. *Indianapolis Museum of Art, Miller House and Garden, Colombus, IN, USA. Design: Daniel Urban Kiley*

MIDDLE LEFT: A rippling fountain in a circular metal receptacle provides an elemental contrast to the surrounding pebbles and drifts of *Stipa tenuissima* (feather grass). *Napa, CA, USA. Design: Topher Delaney*

LEFT: This elegant circular fountain provides a highlight in the gravel hardstanding with a rusted steel edged border and recycled concrete paving in background. *Orinda, CA, USA. Design: Topher Delaney*

RIGHT: A monumental stone bowl overflowing into a hexagonal pool. *Hortus Eystettensis ("The Garden at Eichstätt") Botanical Garden, Germany. 1998 re-creation of original design: Joachim Camerarius and Basilius Besler for Johann Conrad von Gemmingen*

From this brass spout cool water trickles into the stone pool below. *Patio de Los Naranjos, Cordoba, Spain*

A carved stone turtle spouts a jet of water into a stone bowl. *Woljeong-sa Temple, Odaesan, Pyeongchang County, Gangwon Province, South Korea*

A carved stone bird pours water from its beak into a receptacle that flows into a rill below. *Baan Botanica, Bangkok, Thailand. Design: Owner, Bill Bensley*

RIGHT: This triangular polished steel water feature sits in a lawn planted with spring bulbs and reflects the tulips in its base. *Kislingbury, Northamptonshire, England. Design: James Alexander-Sinclair*

FAR RIGHT: A metal zip-shaped pond with burbling water creates an unusual feature inset into this lawn. *Design: Mark Hall*

PAGE RIGHT
CLOCKWISE FROM TOP LEFT:
Contemporary mesh seats are enclosed by a birch stumpery and wooden fence. *The Naturally Fashionable Garden, RHS Chelsea Flower Show 2010. Design: Nicholas Dexter*

Handmade wood and stone seating. "Philosophers Stone" for the "Benchmark" exhibition. *Longhouse Reserve, East Hampton, Long Island, NY, USA. Design: Tom Jahns*

Contemporary wooden chairs on brick paving amongst drift planting of *Molinia caerulea* subsp. *caerulea*, salvia, and nepeta. *"Drifts of Grass", The Walled Garden, Scampston, North Yorkshire, England. Planting design: Piet Oudolf*

Chainsaw-carved wooden bench and table on laid brick patio with *Abutilon megapotamicum* (trailing abutilon) and standard rose bush in container. *Hertfordshire, England. Design: Owner, Kim Wilde*

Brick summerhouse shelter with wooden seats and a pink-flowering climbing rose. *The Madoo Conservancy, Sagaponack, NY, USA. Design: Owner, Robert Dash*

This earthenware bench sits at the end of a line of red posts which draw the eye to an urn at the end of the path and accentuate the distance. Earthenware bench, 2004 by John Utgaard, USA. *"Benchmark" exhibition, Longhouse Reserve, East Hampton, Long Island, NY, USA. Garden design: Owner, Jack Lenor Larsen*

TOP: This circular seating area with oak furniture has a backdrop of a *Prunus laurocerasus* (laurel) hedge. The view looks onto spring-flowering borders with camellia, rhododendron, azalea, and a Japanese maple. *Edinburgh, Scotland. Design: Owner, Mrs. Anne Duncan*

ABOVE: The centrepiece of this pretty suburban spring garden is the white painted metal bench surrounded by large herbaceous perennial borders with many varieties of tulips, *Buxus sempervirens* balls, geranium, bergenia, pittosporum, shrubs, and evergreen hedging. *Edinburgh, Scotland. Design: Owner, Mrs. Anne Duncan*

TOP RIGHT: This relaxed country garden features a rustic wooden bench with living willow pergola and native British meadow planting including *Leucanthemum vulgare* (ox-eye daisy) and *Malva sylvestris* (mallow). *Hertfordshire, England. Design: Owner, Kim Wilde*

Heavy bronze chairs shaded by a striking copper pavilion which contrasts with the foliage of the evergreen *Buxus sempervirens* topiary. *The Laurent Perrier Garden, RHS Chelsea Flower Show 2010, London, England. Garden design: Tom Stuart-Smith; pavilion design: Jamie Fobert Architects*

LEFT TOP: Teak and stainless steel bench, "Diamond Teak". *Longhouse Reserve, East Hampton, Long Island, NY, USA. Design: Barbara and Robert Tiffany*

FAR LEFT: Dressed wood, metal frame, and granite bench. *Tregony, Cornwall, England. Garden design: David Buurma*

LEFT: Pine and steel bench on gravel hardstanding, "Void of Course". *Longhouse Reserve, East Hampton, Long Island, NY, USA. Design: John Houshmand*

ABOVE LEFT: Steel and concrete curving bench set on concrete paving in a contemporary native habitat desert garden. *Baja Canyon garden, Paradise Valley, AZ, USA. Design: Steve Martino*

ABOVE RIGHT: Metal firepit in the centre of a stone and pebble seating area in a coastal contemporary plantsman's garden. *Windcliff, Bainbridge Island, WA, USA. Design: Daniel J. Hinkley and Robert Jones; mosaic design: Jeffrey Bale*

ABOVE : Large curving wooden sculptural bench. Planting includes a border with dahlia, Japanese anemone, heuchera, *Fagus sylvatica* (beech) hedge, and *Prunus* (cherry) trees. *Nursted Barns, Petersfield, Hampshire, England. Design: Acres Wilds; bench design: David Savage*

PAGE LEFT

TOP: This installation of reflective coloured glass panels accentuates its woodland setting. *"Reflexions Colorees", International Garden Festival, Jardin de Metis/Reford Gardens, Quebec, Canada. Design: Hal Ingberg*

BOTTOM LEFT: This textured concrete cone sculpture by French artists Serge and Agnes Bottagisio-Decoux dominates this show garden. Planting includes borage and Jerusalem sage. *"The Saga Insurance Garden", RHS Chelsea Flower Show 2006. Design: Cleve West*

BOTTOM RIGHT: This ball-shaped textured sculpture by French artists Serge and Agnes Bottagisio-Decoux sits in a low reflecting pool of water amongst a border of flowering summer perennials including white-flowering alliums. *The Bupa Garden, RHS Chelsea Flower Show 2008. Design: Cleve West*

RIGHT: A wooden deck allows abstract metal and stone sculptures to be displayed in this modernist garden. *Millstream Sculpture Garden, Bishopstrow, Warminster, Wiltshire, England. House and garden design: Owner, Michael Newberry*

BELOW LEFT: Rusted steel *objets trouvé* make unusual abstract sculptures set against a floor of slates and a backdrop of driftwood. *Lip na Cloiche, Ulva Ferry, Isle of Mull, Argyllshire, Scotland. Design: Owner, Lucy Mackenzie Panizzon*

BELOW RIGHT: Wicker screens covered with climbing plants provide an enclosed space to highlight an abstract stone sculpture. Plants include *Lonicera* (honeysuckle), hebe, and *Hydrangea quercifolia* (oak leaf hydrangea). *Millstream Sculpture Garden, Bishopstrow, Warminster, Wiltshire, England. Garden design: Owner, Michael Newberry*

LEFT: An old metal bathtub makes an ideal trough planter and is softened here with the planting of *Stipa tenuissima* (feather grass). *Hummelo, Holland. Design: Owner, Piet Oudolf*

RIGHT: A reclaimed zinc water tank is used here as a planter for agapanthus and convolvulus. *Tregony, Cornwall. Design: David Buurma*

ABOVE: *Euphorbia cyparissias* and tulips are planted in curving raised beds of yellow painted steel amongst contrasting blue bark chippings. *Der Deutsche Garden, Floriade, Holland, 2002*

BELOW: A city balcony garden uses galvanized metal containers to create a screen of plants. *Islington, London, England. Design: Joe Swift and The Plant Room*

BELOW: Polished steel boxes planted with bamboo make striking containers on this roof garden display. *Regent's Park Flower Show, London, England. Design: Patrick Wynniat-Husey and Patrick Clarke*

ABOVE: Metal rubbish bins look stylish when planted with canna and *Verbena bonariensis. The Dillon Garden, Dublin, Ireland. Design: Owner, Helen Dillon*

BELOW: Shallow geometric concrete containers planted with native cacti and succulents. *Baja Canyon garden, Paradise Valley, Phoenix, AZ, USA. Design: Steve Martino*

ABOVE: This tall ceramic container makes a great display planted with *Libertia grandiflora. The Daily Telegraph Garden, RHS Chelsea Flower Show 2009. Design: Ulf Nordfjell*

ABOVE MIDDLE: A recycled zinc water tank becomes a large rustic planter filled with geranium, pittosporum, and ornamental grasses. *Tregony, Cornwall. Design: David Buurma*

ABOVE RIGHT: A rustic half oak barrel is planted with *Rhus* (sumach) and *Tropaeolum majus* (nasturtium). *Hertfordshire, England. Design: Owner, Kim Wilde*

RIGHT: Wheelbarrows planted with a mix of herbaceous perennials and shrubs make unusual and moveable containers. *International Garden Festival, Jardin de Metis/Reford Gardens, Quebec, Canada*

TOP: A mix of glazed and mosaic planters, walls and paving make a colourful impact in this small city garden. Planting includes fatsia, pelargonium, *Laurus nobilis* (bay), and magnolia. *London, England. Design: Owner, Kaffe Fassett*

ABOVE LEFT: Smooth surfaced, light-coloured ceramic urns planted with citrus trees contrast with the textured foliage of libertia. *Orinda, CA, USA. Design: Topher Delaney/SEAM Studio*

LEFT: This paved area of lush jungle garden uses a mixture of containers to complement a mass of eclectic plants including pseudopanax, yucca, and ornamental grasses. *Berkeley, CA, USA. Design: Former owners, Roger Raiche and David McCrory*

ABOVE: Dark coloured ceramic containers contrast with *Petunia* 'Limelight' and verbena in this pretty country garden. *Alchemilla mollis* (lady's mantle) softens the edges. *Ardentinny, Argyllshire, Scotland. Design: Owners, Barry and Freda Waldapfel*

ABOVE: Elegant terracotta pots filled with *Cyperus papyrus* (papyrus) reflect in the still water of the rill in this Mediterranean-style courtyard garden. *Chanticleer Garden, PA, USA. Garden design: Chris Woods; planting design: Dan Benarcik*

LEFT: A variety of terracotta containers display drought-tolerant succulents, evergreen trees and flowering perennials, including *Aeonium arboreum* 'Zwartkop', aloes, and agave. *Heronswood Nursery, Bainsbridge Island, WA, USA. Design: Owners, Daniel J. Hinkley and Robert Jones*

ABOVE RIGHT: A regimented line of terracotta pots filled with *Aeonium* 'Zwartkop' make a bold statement in this contemporary Mediterranean garden. *"The Black Work", Le Jardin de l'Alchimiste, Eygalieres en Provence, France. Design: Arnaud Maurières and Éric Ossart*

RIGHT: An orderly selection of succulent and alpine plants in small terracotta pots are placed in a wooden tray to create an artistic display. *Ardentinny, Argyllshire, Scotland. Design: Owners, Barry and Freda Waldapfel*

LEFT: Terracotta planters filled with boxwood balls make a graphic display against the backdrop of a flowering camellia and windows of this elegant conservatory. *Lancaster, Lancashire, England. Design: David Redmore*

TOP LEFT: Branches tied with twine make ideal sweet pea tepees and rustic features. *Kelmarsh Hall and Walled Garden, Northampton, Northamptonshire, England. Planting design: Esther McMillan*

ABOVE LEFT: This cool blue painted pergola stands above pretty mosaics and steps to make an elegant entrance to the a rill and pond. *Shepherd House Garden, Inveresk, Midlothian, Scotland. Design: Owners, Sir Charles and Lady Ann Fraser. Sculpture: Gerald Laing*

LEFT: A swimming pool terrace is given a large wooden pergola for climbing plants to provide welcome shade on hot summer days. *Salem, NY, USA. Design: Oehme, van Sweden*

TOP: Pale blue painted wooden obelisk plant supports make a pretty framework for sweet peas to grow up and provide height in this vegetable garden. *Columbine Hall, Stowmarket, Suffolk, England. Design: Owners, Hew Stevenson and Leslie Geddes-Brown*

ABOVE: This gothic-style wooden pergola performs a variety of functions. Primarily a framework for a seating area surrounded by *Carpinus betulus* (hornbeam) trees it also acts as a support for climbing plants. *Holywell Hall, Lincolnshire, England. Design: Bunny Guinness*

LEFT: Bold contemporary metalwork complements the inner city surroundings. Stainless steel curves create an archway while metal fencing and wire provide the support needed for climbing plants. *Jardin Atlantique, Gare Montparnasse, Paris. Design: Francois Brun and Michel Pena*

BELOW LEFT AND BELOW: Various climbing plants are each given space for their display on galvanized metal supports – the close-up shows tendrils of *Wisteria macrostachya* 'Aunt Dee'. *M. Victor and Frances Leventritt Garden, The Arnold Arboretum of Harvard University, Boston, MA, USA. Design: Reed Hilderbrand*

ABOVE: Brightly coloured hand painted plant pots filled with herbs are clearly labelled on this city apartment window ledge. *London, England*

BELOW: Old metal sign letters make a humorous phrase on the fence of this vegetable garden. *Portland, OR, USA. Design: Owners, Steven J. Maker and Harvey W. Freer*

ABOVE: Terracotta pots are used here to display the house number, placed on a rustic wooden bench with curved rusted rebars surrounded by plants: *Cupressus macrocarpa* 'Goldcrest' (Monterey cypress, lemon cypress) and hebe. *Mesembryanthenum* is planted in the gravel below. *Portland, OR, USA. Design: Owner, Nancy Goldman*

BELOW: This cast concrete sign clearly marks the entrance to these Victorian glasshouses. *Crathes Castle Garden and Estate, Banchory, Aberdeenshire, Scotland*

ABOVE: Razor clam shells are used as labels for cuttings of *Ozothamnus rosmarinifolius* 'Silver Jubilee' in this pretty seaside nursery. *Lip na Cloiche Garden and Nursery, Isle of Mull, Argyllshire, Scotland. Design: Owner, Lucy Mackenzie Panizzon*

RIGHT: This shrub area of the nursery is identified by a handmade and painted driftwood sign. *Lip na Cloiche Garden and Nursery, Isle of Mull, Argyllshire, Scotland. Design: Owner, Lucy Mackenzie Panizzon*

FAR RIGHT: This sweet, delicate sign is ceramic with a metal edge and support. It is set amongst flowers and seed heads of *Nigella damascena* (Love-in-a-mist). *Hertfordshire, England. Garden design: Owner, Kim Wilde*

RIGHT: Decorative labels with handwritten wishes hang from the branches of a *Sorbus* (rowan) tree in this community garden. *The Hidden Gardens, Glasgow, Scotland. Design: nva organisation and City Design Cooperative*

ABOVE LEFT: An oriental-style wooden bridge doubles as a shelter and romantic sitting area. *The Madoo Conservancy, Sagaponack, NY, USA. Design: Owner, Robert Dash*

ABOVE: This wooden, thatched gazebo has open sides to enjoy the tropical climate in this Caribbean coastal garden. It is positioned within a shelter belt of *Coccoloba uvifera* (sea grape) and palm trees. *Barbados. Design: Owner, Kevin Talma*

LEFT: A wooden summerhouse with metal roof has the benefit of a porch for New England chairs, providing a comfortable seating solution. *Landenberg, PA, USA. Design: Owners, Rick Darke and Melinda Zoehrer*

RIGHT: This glazed wooden summerhouse is shaded by an apple tree in full blossom and makes a restful shelter. *Summerdale Garden, Lupton, Cumbria, England. Garden design: Owners, David and Gail Sheals*

FAR RIGHT: A fern-shaded area in the bottom of a suburban garden is a perfect setting for an artist's studio. *Twickenham, Surrey, England. Design: Owner, Ian Sidaway*

RIGHT: This stone-walled flower house is an idyllic cool place to prepare cut flowers for the rooms inside this Italian Villa. *Borgo Santo Pietro, Chiusdino, Italy. Design: Owners, Jeanette and Claus Thottrup*

FAR RIGHT: A wooden-framed hexagonal summerhouse with leaded windows provides a hidden shelter amongst ferns and ornamental grasses. *Bourne, Lincolnshire, England. Garden design: Owners, Ivan and Sadie Hall*

FAR LEFT: This wooden summerhouse with log store is painted in a Scandinavian grey to complement the warm tones of the gravel path and ceramic containers. *Ardentinny, Argyllshire, Scotland. Design: Owners, Barry and Freda Waldapfel*

LEFT: This small stone hut is recognizably British with its red telephone box. Colourful planting includes *Verbascum* (mullein), *Euphorbia* (spurge), iris, *Aquilegia* (columbine), and delphiniums. *"Yorkshire Alive with Opportunity", RHS Chelsea Flower Show 2003. Design: Julian Dowle*

FAR LEFT BELOW: This wooden shed is concealed within a well-stocked country garden. The boxwood hedges contain a herb bed with *Mentha* (mint), *Rosmarinus officinalis* (rosemary), and a standard pink-flowering rose. *Lonicera* (honeysuckle) and *Akebia quinata* (chocolate vine) are climbing the trellis. *Hertfordshire, England. Design: Kim Wilde*

LEFT BELOW: A darkly painted wooden hut adorned with bird houses is concealed in an area of birch woodland in this community garden. *The Hidden Gardens, Glasgow, Scotland. Design: nva organisation and City Design Cooperative*

PAGE RIGHT
TOP LEFT: Tool sheds for gardeners are painted in warm tones of green to blend amongst foliage of the woods and wildflower meadow. *International Garden Festival, Jardin de Metis/Reford Gardens, Quebec, Canada*

TOP RIGHT: A sweet little wooden outhouse with a moon shape cut into the door. *Skagit Valley, WA, USA. Design: Owners, Dick and Lavone Reim*

RIGHT: Wooden outbuildings in this woodland garden are surrounded by shade-loving plants, including ferns and *Astilboides tabularis*. *The Madoo Conservancy, Sagaponack, NY, USA. Design: Owner, Robert Dash*

ABOVE: A triangular glazed structure is attached to the back of an historic red brick building to act as a potting shed and glasshouse. *Kelmarsh Hall and Walled Garden, Northamptonshire, England. Planting design: Esther MacMillan*

RIGHT: A large and impressive conservatory building designed by Marston and Langinger for a formal suburban garden. It is complemented by terracotta pots filled with *Buxus sempervirens* balls. *Lancaster, Lancashire, England. Garden design: David Redmore*

FAR RIGHT: The glasshouse is the focal point of this coastal, country garden. Stone steps lead to its entrance through a painted wooden picket fence and flanked with *Erigeron karvankianus* (Mexican fleabane) and *Centranthus ruber* (Valerian, Jupiter's beard). *Lip na Cloiche, Ulva Ferry, Isle of Mull, Argyllshire, Scotland. Garden design: Owner, Lucy Mackenzie Panizzon*

MIDDLE LEFT: Here a small, unobtrusive aluminium and glass greenhouse does not distract from the prettiness of the poppies, marigolds, and vegetables growing in the raised bed around it. *Shropshire, England. Design: Owner, Jenny Goodrich*

MIDDLE RIGHT: This large Victorian glasshouse was built against the bricks of the walled garden in what used to be Chesters Walled Garden Nursery. *Hexham, Northumberland, England. Garden design: Susie White*

BELOW RIGHT: This grand Victorian-style glasshouse in a walled garden grows ornamental plants as well as vegetables and herbs for a restaurant. *Loch Lomond Golf Club, Rossdhu House, Dunbartonshire, Scotland. Design: Alitex*

FAR RIGHT: The beauty of this carefully restored Victorian fernery is mostly below ground where it is filled with a notable collection of ferns amongst pretty water pools. Outside it is surrounded by herbaceous perennial borders. *Ascog Hall Gardens, Isle of Bute, Argyllshire, Scotland. Restoration: the late Wallace and Katherine Fyfe. Garden design: Graham and Susannah Alcorn*

TOP LEFT: The glasshouse here provides a centrepiece for a minimal maintenance, eco-friendly, and organic garden. The decking is made from recycled material and ceramic containers include planting of a spiky *Astelia chathamica*. *"Halls Trilogy Garden", RHS Chelsea Flower Show 2003. Design: Spinneywell Consortium*

ABOVE: A conservatory can provide not just an elegant setting for semi-tropical plants, but also an elegant eating place. *Lancaster, Lancashire, England. Conservatory design: Marston and Langinger. Planting design: David Redmore*

LEFT: Wooden framed glazed conservatory provides a wonderful setting for breakfast with a clear view over the productive gardens at this former restaurant and hotel. *Scholteshof, Hasselt, Belgium*

TOP LEFT: Here design has been used as a statement about the effects of global warming and greenhouse gases on our environment. Ponds of algae run through three greenhouses made of wood and transparent plastic. *"L'Effet Desert"*, *International Garden Festival, Jardin de Metis/Reford Gardens, Quebec, Canada.* Design: Eric Daoust, Donald Potvin, and Jean-François Potvin

LEFT: A simple aluminium and glass cold frame houses a range of young plants including zucchini, basil, and parsley. *Supplier: crocus.co.uk*

TOP RIGHT: This skeletal glasshouse installation is made from scaffolding poles and decorated with recycled glass bottles and builders bags planted with herbal trees. *"Glasshouse", Orangerie, Gothenberg Garden Festival 2008, Gunnebo House and Gardens, Sweden.* Design: Topher Delaney

ABOVE: This contemporary wood and glass pavilion uses metal for seating and an ornamental grill. Metallic planters also contain *Libertia grandiflora* and the backdrop is provided by a *Carpinus betulus* hedge. *The Daily Telegraph Garden, RHS Chelsea Flower Show 2009.* Design: Ulf Nordfjell

SPACE

"Let every house be placed, if the person pleases, in the middle of its plot . . . so there may be ground on each side for gardens or orchards or fields, that it may be a green country town, which will never be burnt and always be wholesome."

William Penn, the Quaker and founder of Pennsylvania, was here referring to the layout of the city of Philadelphia in 1682, giving advice to the first settlers. This ideal of every individual property being surrounded by plentiful green space is sadly not always feasible. We have to work with what we have, be it a country estate or an urban window box.

Possibly the hardest part of owning a garden space is not filling it. Many of the best garden designers are known for their restraint. Adding extras can be all too tempting. And I can say that from a photographer's perspective less is definitely more.

It is always important to consider what is actually wanted from a particular space. What features could benefit from being outdoors instead of inside the house? For individuals and families the answers to this vary enormously, but it seems crucial for a designer to listen hard to the answers. The next challenge is how to incorporate the requirements to the space available within the constraints of environment and budget. Functional elements also need to be considered whether for entertaining friends and family, playing sports, or growing vegetables.

A recent visit to a friend's tiny garden impressed me. She had used the space available thoughtfully to make a place for sitting, somewhere to escape to where you could read and relax. Despite having two children there were no signs of play areas or spaces to run around in. Instead, this was a quiet place to come home to from school or work. A short walk away there was plenty of space for play – a park for the kids and equally close by a community garden for her own growing of plants – so all needs were catered for.

Limited space makes the task of design very challenging. Devices can be used to give the feeling of more space than there actually is. For example, screens can section off areas whilst light colours can open up a dark corner. Changing levels can also add to the feeling of space.

Cultural differences too can influence the way space is used. The American view of space historically has been towards the landscape – or wilderness – beyond. For that reason few garden fences can be seen around garden plots even in towns in the United States. Gardens are open and outward looking. In Europe historically vistas have been focussed on the landowners' own buildings and land. As garden writer Tim Richardson explains in *Great Gardens of America*: "In America, even in cases where the detail of the design was originally inspired by European examples, it seems that the beckoning natural landscape will often be harnessed to set the tone of the garden as a whole. Vistas in America for example can just as often be wide and general as opposed to object- or building-focussed, as they are in Europe. This lends many of these gardens an expansive, unbounded feel, quite at odds with the European tradition, where an attempt is often made to fence out wilderness by means of enclosures."

Any personal space is to be cherished, whether it be borrowed vistas or open landscapes. Providing space for children to play and enjoy will provide them with happy memories and encourage a further generation of sensitive caretakers of our precious outdoor spaces. Enclosed by walls or shaded by trees, gardens of any size or locality, urban or rural, shaded or exposed, have the potential to give so much pleasure if thought through with vision – whether inward- or outward-looking.

RIGHT: Potager Garden, Lincolnshire, England. Design: Paul Thompson and Ann-Marie Powell

LEFT: The swirling design of this back garden maximizes the space and allows room for dining and relaxing whilst a summerhouse stores all the tools. *Phyllostachys nigra* and *Dicksonia antarctica* (Tasmanian tree fern) add a jungly look to the planting. *London, England. Design: Joe Swift and The Plant Room*

MIDDLE: A galvanized metal balcony and steps lead to this London back garden camouflaged by abundant trees and shrubs. *Camden, London, England. Design: Owner, Dale Loth*

RIGHT: In this tiny urban space a tranquil Japanese-style garden has been created with ponds, paving stones, and steps surrounded by a mix of mosses and textured foliage. *Holland. Design: Owner, Geert Jansen*

PAGE LEFT

TOP: Here a walled London garden is disguised by country styling. The thatched wooden shelter and decking look over the natural-looking pond in front of which stands a specimen *Corylus avellana* 'Contorta' (corkscrew hazel). *Chiswick, London, England. Design: Matt Vincent*

MIDDLE: This walled urban space has been transformed into a lush water garden using reclaimed railway sleepers (railroad ties) and architectural planting such as *Dicksonia antarctica* (Tasmanian tree fern), *Pittosporum tobira*, *Hedychium* (ginger lily), and *Equisetum* (horsetail). *Hampstead, London, England. Planting design: Jason Payne*

BOTTOM: The approach to this suburban garden is made inviting by a generous planting of herbaceous perennials in the "hell strip", including *Lavandula stoechas* (French lavender), *Cistus* (rock rose), geranium, *Kniphofia* (red hot poker), *Nepeta* (catmint), and roses. *Portland, OR, USA. Design: Owner, Nancy Goldman*

TOP LEFT: This elegant townhouse uses a gravel border to grow plants with varying heights such as *Dierama pulcherrimum* (angel's fishing rod), *Euphorbia* (spurge), sanguisorba, and ferns. *The Dillon Garden, Dublin, Ireland. Design: Owner, Helen Dillon*

TOP RIGHT: Exotic planting in the front garden makes this regular home on an estate appear as if in a tropical oasis. Architectural planting includes echium, hardy palms, agave, junipers, pines, *Acer* (Japanese maple), and *Cordyline* (cabbage palm). *Norwich, Norfolk, England. Design: Owner, Jon Kelf*

ABOVE: A wooden built outdoor eating area gives this brick house an extra dimension. Container planting and topiary decorate the patio giving a green feel – *Hosta* 'June' in metal containers. *Bourne, Lincolnshire, England. Design: Owners, Ivan and Sadie Hall*

ABOVE: This urban garden is designed to be shared by a number of residents with completely different needs. The transition is made from deck to lawn then to planted gravel garden and barbecue area at the back. *Lewisham, London, England. Design: Ann-Marie Powell and Paul Thompson*

PAGE LEFT
FAR LEFT: This town garden gives the impression of infinite space as the snaking slate wall leads your eye by means of a gravel path around a cherry tree away from the house. *Putney, London, England. Design: Roberto Silva*

LEFT: A graduation of gravel, pebbles, and rocks are used to create this manmade stream which winds its way through this front garden in suburbia planted with alpines and ornamental grasses. *England. Design: Owners*

ABOVE: The centrepiece of this elegant town garden is a water canal flanked by tall herbaceous perennials highlighted with repeat planting of pink and fluffy *Filipendula rubra* 'Venusta'. *The Dillon Garden, Dublin, Ireland. Design: Owner, Helen Dillon*

LEFT ABOVE: The use of tall ornamental grasses and late summer flowering perennials blend well with the countryside landscape during harvest time. *Lower Foxhanger, Somerset, England. Design: James Alexander-Sinclair*

LEFT MIDDLE: Wood and bricks make a stage for the flowering plants in terracotta pots amid a gravel bed. *Myosotis* (forget-me-not) and *Aquilegia* (columbine) soften the edges. *Portland, OR, USA. Design: Owners, Steven J. Maker and Harvey W. Freer*

LEFT BOTTOM: Within this spacious country garden swathes of ornamental grasses, *Perovskia* (Russian sage), and *Lavandula* (lavender) conceal a wooden bench in a gravel area secluded by a beech hedge. *Hampshire, England. Design: Acres Wild*

ABOVE: Terracotta urns and pots feature in this walled country garden with a brick-built summerhouse. Boxwood hedging surrounds a lawn punctuated with fruit trees. *Hampshire, England. Design: Garden owner*

ABOVE: This converted barn with a wooden pergola is complemented by beds of lush perennial foliage enclosed by brick-edged gravel paths. Planting includes *Acanthus mollis, Foeniculum vulgare* (fennel), *Cynara cardunculus* (cardoon), wisteria, and rose climbers. *Hertfordshire, England. Design: Owner, Kim Wilde*

RIGHT ABOVE: A shelterbelt of tall poplar trees protect this vintage wooden barn. *Cynara cardunculus* (cardoon) are planted in the foreground. *Mount Vernon, Skagit Valley, WA, USA. Design: Owners, Dick and Lavone Reim*

RIGHT: An ornamental *Prunus* (cherry) tree full of spring blossom gives the shade required to bluebells around a stone seat in this country garden. *Mount Vernon, Skagit Valley, WA, USA. Design: Owners, Dick and Lavone Reim*

FAR RIGHT: This country garden makes good use of shrubs and trees, giving plenty of variety in height. The foliage and spring blossom provide colour and texture. The white-flowering viburnum in the foreground is particularly stunning. *Mount Vernon, Skagit Valley, WA, USA. Design: Owners, Dick and Lavone Reim*

ABOVE: Cast rendered concrete paving contrasts here with natural stone boulders providing a stunning setting for a rill between ponds in this waterside plantsman's garden. Eclectic planting includes *Lobelia tupa, Cortaderia fulvida, Dierama pulcherrimum, Butia capitata,* cacti, and *Stipa tenuissima. Bainbridge Island, WA, USA. Design: Owners, Daniel J. Hinkley and Robert Jones*

LEFT: A gravel path runs through this coastal garden on the cliffs above the English Channel. *Oenothera biennis,* lavender, *Alchemilla mollis, Lychnis coronaria,* gypsophila, euphorbia, and roses all feature in these colourful borders. *Dawlish, Devon, England. Design: Owner, Naila Green*

RIGHT TOP: Varieties of narcissus are planted here in the lawn with a view to Loch Ewe. *Inverewe (NTS), Wester Ross, Scotland. Original Garden Design: Sir Osgood Mackenzie*

RIGHT MIDDLE: Decking provides a platform here for a secluded suntrap in this garden on cliffs above the English Channel. *Dawlish, Devon, England. Design: Owner, Naila Green*

RIGHT BOTTOM: This Mediterranean-style coastal terrace garden slopes towards the sea. Tough and spiky drought-tolerant plants include agave, yucca, cordyline, and *Trachycarpus fortunei. Lamorran House Gardens, St. Mawes, Cornwall, England. Design: Owner, Robert Dudley-Cooke*

LEFT TOP: Neo-classical columns provide an unusual perimeter to a seating area looking over the sea view. Surrounding plants include agave and hardy palms. *Lamorran House Gardens, St. Mawes, Cornwall, England. Design: Owner, Robert Dudley-Cooke*

LEFT MIDDLE: *Papaver rhoeas* grow wild on the cliff tops in the south coast of England. *Dawlish, Devon, England*

LEFT: This seaside garden looks out towards the island of Ulva. The kitchen garden is sheltered by trees and shrubs.

Lip na Cloiche Garden and Nursery, Isle of Mull, Argyllshire, Scotland. Design: Owner, Lucy Mackenzie Panizzon

ABOVE: This steeply sloping coastal garden boasts a wooden summerhouse which looks out towards the Puget Sound. Plants around the bark chipping path include a mix of flowering rhododendrons, herbaceous perennials, spring bulbs, shrubs, and evergreen trees. *Seattle, WA, USA. Design: Owners, Lynn and Ralph Davis*

ABOVE : Concrete rendering with large boulders create a natural-looking area extending this seaside garden to the very edge of the water. Foliage and flower are *Carpobrotus edulis* (highway ice plant) – not introduced by the designer, but an escapee from planting in the late 1960s/early 1970s. *Santa Barbara, CA, USA. Design: Isabelle Greene*

PAGE LEFT

LEFT: This tiny basement courtyard garden has a tropical feel. Beds surrounding slate tile flooring are filled with bamboos and a *Musa basjoo* (banana tree). *Islington, London, England. Design: Joe Swift and The Plant Room*

RIGHT ABOVE: A metal pergola leads into this small stone-cobbled courtyard where a little buxus topiary is the centrepiece. Plants include *Hydrangea quercifolia* (oakleaf hydrangea) in the background with *Rosa* 'Danse de Feu' and *Lonicera* (honeysuckle) climbing the archway. *Hertfordshire, England. Design: Owner, Kim Wilde*

RIGHT BELOW: A fun tiny contemporary decking garden is sheltered by wooden walls with multi-coloured metal wall planters filled with edible herb and salad plants. *The PSI Nursery Garden, RHS Chelsea Flower Show 2009. Design: Jamie Dunstan*

THIS PAGE

TOP: This small courtyard garden is enclosed by clean white walls. It uses a combination of wooden decking and tiles for the flooring and the raised beds are filled with bold plants such as *Phyllostachys nigra, Phormium* (New Zealand flax), *Miscanthus sinensis* 'Zebrinus' (zebra grass), and *Dicksonia antarctica* (Tasmanian tree fern). *Barnes, London, England. Design: Joe Swift and The Plant Room*

BOTTOM: A contemporary city front garden with wood-clad building uses eco-friendly elements such as rainwater recycling and porous paving. The raised bed is planted with perennials including allium, geum, *Phormium tenax*, salvia, and iris growing in gravel. Beside the door is a square white raised bed with *Luma apiculata. "Urban Rain", RHS Chelsea Flower Show 2008. Design: Bob Latham*

PAGE LEFT
TOP: A quiet green sanctuary is created by using wooden raised beds and planted trellis to soften the rear brick wall. Bricks and tiles are mixed to provide pattern in the flooring. Structure to the planting is provided by *Phormium tenax*, *Buxus sempervirens*, and *Lavandula stoechas* and filled in between with *Salvia officinalis*, *Rosmarinus officinalis*, *Vinca major*, and *Helichrysum italicum*. *Brixton, London, England. Design: Paul Thompson with Ann-Marie Powell*

MIDDLE: This small paved courtyard garden uses brick to enclose the low raised beds and terracotta-style containers to house mixed planting. Overhanging is a *Pyrus* (pear) tree with fruit and in the bed *Eriobotrya japonica*

(loquat), *Phormium* (New Zealand flax), agapathus, and *Pittosporum tobira*. Containers house a variegated yucca and *Pennisetum* (ornamental grass). *Camden, London, England. Design: Paul Thompson*

BOTTOM LEFT: This paved courtyard in central London offers a quiet outdoor eating place. Mesh metal fencing makes a great support for the fragrant *Trachelospermum jasminoides* (star jasmine). Planted below are *Lavandula stoechas* (French lavender), *Buxus sempervirens* balls, variegated *Hedera* (ivy), *Vitis vinfera* (grape), and *Laurus nobilis* (bay). *Waterloo, London, England. Design: Gerhard Jenner*

BOTTOM RIGHT: White-flowering *Galega officinalis* climbs the brick wall here in this small country garden. A pile of rusted horseshoes makes an unusual ornament beside an old cart wheel. Underplanting includes *Alchemilla mollis* and *Geranium psilostemon*. *Bourne, Lincolnshire, England. Design: Owners, Ivan and Sadie Hall*

ABOVE: This country-style courtyard back garden is in the outskirts of London. The wooden summerhouse and pergola all add to the rustic look, whereas the all-in-one stone-look table and bench are designed by Conran and adds a touch of urban style. Herbs and grasses are planted in the gravel bed between the wooden planks. *Richmond, Surrey, England. Design: Wayne Page*

ABOVE: This London roof garden uses metal containers to house planting of standard variegated *Ilex* (holly), *Alchemila mollis*, heuchera, euphorbia, *Rosmarinus officinalis*, hosta, hebe, and *Stipa tenuissima* (feather grass). *Notting Hill, London, England. Design: Robin and Jacqui Stubbs*

LEFT: A contemporary eco-friendly roof garden that uses a "leaky pipe" to irrigate the planting in gravel beds. The main area is concrete paving, while the outer perimeter is fenced for safety with a metal grill. Planting includes sedum, salvia, lavander, and achillea. *USA's First LEED Homes Platinum Residential Duplex Project, Philadelphia, PA, USA. Design: Onion Flats*

RIGHT TOP: Often city roof gardens will be exposed to high winds. Here stainless steel trough planters contain windproof *Phormium* (New Zealand flax) and *Festuca glauca* (blue fescue). *The Piper Building, Fulham, London, England. Planting Design: Matt Vincent*

BELOW: Wooden decking can be used to create steps and seating. Metal planters are filled with *Laurus nobilis* (bay), miscanthus, *Lavandula* (lavender), and *Rosmarinus* officinalis (rosemary). *London, England. Design: Paul Thompson*

ABOVE : Here a contemporary urban roof garden keeps cool under sail shades. Wooden panels minimize wind and street noise. *Clerkenwell, London, England. Design Paul Thompson and Ann-Marie Powell*

RIGHT: This small chic roof garden is made with wooden decking. Galvanized metal planters are filled with silver-leaved *Convolvulus cneorum* and bamboo. Colour is introduced through the soft furnishings and accessories. *Islington, London, England. Design: Joe Swift and The Plant Room*

FAR RIGHT: *Verbena bonariensis* gives a veil of height and colour to the raised beds in this small roof top garden. *Islington, London, England. Design: Joe Swift and The Plant Room*

ABOVE: This domestic flat roof is planted as a miniature gravel garden with drought-tolerant grasses and low-growing perennials. *Gloucestershire, England. Design: Owner*

ABOVE RIGHT: A home office with a green roof planted thickly with sedums. A chain rainwater catcher to aid drainage adds a further element to this eco-friendly design. *"The Help the Aged SoHo Garden", RHS Chelsea Flower Show 2003. Design: Mark Gregory*

RIGHT: A city vegetative roof insulates, cools, handles storm water, and doubles the life of the roof. It also reduces the urban heat island effect. *Friends Center, Philadelphia, PA, USA. Design: Roofscapes Inc.*

MIDDLE LEFT: A domestic garage roof planted as a wildflower meadow making a colourful interlude to the monotony of a housing estate. *Germany. Design: Owner, Dr. Gunther Mann*

LEFT: Naturalistic planting disguises the fact that this roof garden is on the top floor of an apartment block. *Simaringen, Germany*

ABOVE: This residential living roof is part of a complete working project developed to increase awareness of sustainable landscape possibilities. *Elmhurst, IL, USA. Design: Owner, Marcus de la Fleur*

ABOVE: This cafe courtyard garden features small coloured glass beads inset into the concrete paving. The metal framed awning provides shelter from the elements if needed. *Vitis vinifera* (grape), *Phyllostachys nigra*, and *Humulus lupulus* 'Aureus' (golden hop) all help to provide seclusion through their foliage of varied textures and colours. *WXD Cafe, Crouch End, London, England. Design: Dan Pearson and Steve Bradley*

LEFT: A narrow rill with fountain zig zags its way through this courtyard garden. The white-painted brick wall creates a clean look and wooden screen fencing on the left adds warmth and a good support for climbers. The flowering *Cornus* (dogwood) takes centrestage in summer whilst the red and gold foliage of *Liquidambar styraciflua* (American sweetgum) gleams in autumn. *Paddington, London, England. Design: James Alexander-Sinclair*

RIGHT: A swimming pool flanked by *Cryptomeria japonica* underplanted with *Hakonechloa macra* features in this American town garden. *Georgetown, Washington, DC, USA. Design: Oehme, van Sweden*

LEFT ABOVE: Wood-framed French doors open the inside of this townhouse into the contemporary hardscaped space outside. Within the raised beds are *Phyllostachys nigra*, phormium, *Miscanthus sinensis* 'Zebrinus', and a *Dicksonia antarctica* (tree fern). *London, England. Design: Joe Swift and The Plant Room*

LEFT: This large wall of sliding windows unites the house with the lawn where a ceramic sculpture features against the woodland backdrop. *Orinda, CA, USA. Landscape Design: Topher Delaney*

ABOVE: This minimalist glass conservatory with kitchen surfaces and floor paving extends the space into a garden planted with just *Phyllostachys nigra* (black bamboo). *London, England. Design: Green Target Design*

RIGHT: Folding large French doors draw the eye out of the house and into this garden. The outside surface is a combination of decking and slate paving which leads to a summerhouse and chunky wooden fence. *London, England. Design: Joe Swift and The Plant Room*

FAR LEFT: Flowing curtains give a light and summery feel to this view through French doors to the potager garden. The shape of the window frames is echoed by the painted wooden pergola beyond. *Spalding, Lincolnshire, England. Design: Paul Thompson with Ann-Marie Powell*

LEFT: Doors from the living room lead out onto this paved city courtyard garden. To soften the urban view *Clematis armandii* is planted over the metal pergola. *London, England. Design: Owner, Gerhard Jenner*

FAR LEFT: This patterned glazed doorway leads from a dark and shady interior to a light paved garden area surrounded by dense foliage of phyllostachys and *Magnolia grandiflora*. The stone paving is intersected with dark pebbles and leads to a conservatory at rear of garden. *Georgetown, Washington, DC, USA. Design: Oehme, van Sweden*

LEFT: Muted tones of pale grey/blue link the outside with the interior of this smart coastal residence. Outside chunky zinc plant containers are filled with dark-leaved pittosporum and pale pink-flowering geranium. *Tregony, Cornwall, England. Design: David Buurma*

RIGHT: This basement bedroom is glazed to allow any available light in from the shady courtyard garden. Impressively large leaves of *Musa basjoo* feature in the planting outside. *London, England. Garden design: Joe Swift and The Plant Room*

BELOW: This elegant sun room has sliding French doors leading out to spring-flowering borders. *Lancaster, Lancashire, England. Design: David Redmore*

BELOW RIGHT: Bathroom doors open into this small garden of shade and damp-loving plants, including equisetum, ferns, sedges, and ophiopogon. *Portland, OR, USA. Design: Owners, Norm Kalbfleisch and Neil Matteucci*

TOP LEFT: This large walled potager garden is broken up with lawn paths, edged with flowering lavender. A sweet pea tepee sits in the bed opposite a wall of green beans. *Holywell Hall, Lincolnshire, England. Design: Bunny Guinness*

TOP RIGHT: The outer wall of this garden is softened with trained fruit trees and climbing roses. Pink-flowering *Nerine bowdenii* (nerine) line the foot of the wall. *Cambo Walled Garden, Fife, Scotland. Design: Owner, Lady Catherine Erskine and head gardener, Elliot Forsyth*

LEFT: This converted old barn and farmyard are planted with colourful herbaceous perennial borders. Statuesque ornamental grasses create a backdrop for salvia, geum, *Papaver orientale, Melianthus major* (honey bush), sisyrinchium, and *Foeniculum vulgare* (fennel). *Blackpitts Farm, Northamptonshire, England. Design: Owner, James Alexander-Sinclair*

ABOVE: This border is in a sheltered spot outside the walled garden where light catches allium seedheads dotted amongst the *Nepeta* (catmint). *Kelmarsh Hall and Walled Garden, Northamptonshire, England. Design: Esther McMillan*

TOP: A brick wall provides support and shelter for flowering perennials, evergreen shrubs, and climbers. Planting includes *Euonymus fortunei*, *Ilex aquifolium* 'Elegantissima', *Viburnum carlesii*, Clematis, *Helleborus foetidus* (stinking hellebore), and peony. *The Liz Christy Community Garden, Manhattan, New York, NY, USA. Design: The Community Gardeners*

ABOVE: Here planting includes hosta varieties, zantedeschia, gunnera, *Rheum* (ornamental rhubarb), rhododendrons, *Polygonatum* (Solomon's seal). *The Walled Garden at Crug Farm Plants Nursery, Caernarfon, Gwynned, Wales. Design: Bleddyn and Sue Wynn-Jones*

PAGE RIGHT

TOP: In this 1930 re-creation of an original 1604 design a walled garden features stone panels depicting the Seven Cardinal Virtues, the Seven Liberal Arts, and the Seven Planetary Deities. Buxus and yew hedging, lawns with rose beds. *Edzell Castle Gardens, Brechin, Angus, Scotland*

MIDDLE: A worn wooden door leads through the snow into this sheltered brick walled garden protecting an old espaliered fruit tree and buxus hedging. *The Walled Garden, Caprington Castle, Kilmarnock, Ayrshire, Scotland*

FAR RIGHT: Stylish wicker compost bins blend with the gentle colour of Cotswold-stone walls supporting espaliered fruit trees and climbing roses. *The Daylesford Organic "Summer Solstice" Garden, RHS Chelsea Flower Show 2008. Design: Tommaso del Buono and Paul Gazerwitz*

RIGHT: In this walled garden trained apple fruit trees contrast against a red brick wall. *Hampshire, England*

ABOVE: Walled potager garden with lawns, orchard, trained fruit trees, herb garden, *Buxus sempervirens* hedge and balls, white tulips, urns, and summerhouse. Trained *Pyrus* (pear) trees grow against the wall. *Hampshire, England*

TOP: Here a small London garden is planted as a woodland area giving shade and tranquility. Trees and shrubs used include *Acer palmatum* var. *heptalobum*, *Cotinus coggygria*, hebe, and camellia. *Camden, London, England. Design: Owner, Dale Loth*

MIDDLE: This shady spring garden has a central small lawn surrounded by a planting of richly textured perennial plants, shrubs, and deciduous trees. The inner ring includes maianthemum, hosta, pulmonaria, azalea, rhododendron, and polygonatum. *Sweden. Design: Roland and Eva Gustavsson*

BOTTOM LEFT: Gravel paths wind through this shady walled garden. The large leaves of gunnera provide ultimate cover over a lower layer of sanguisorba, hosta, lilium, rheum, zantedeschia, and ferns. *Crug Farm Plants, Wales. Design: Owners, Bleddyn and Sue Wynn-Jones*

BOTTOM RIGHT: Overhanging tree branches create shade for a wattle seat in this country garden. *Buckinghamshire, England. Design: Channel 4 Garden Doctors, Steve Bradley and Dan Pearson*

LEFT: Fallen tree trunks, moss, ferns, *Lysichiton americanus* (western skunk cabbage), and wiry huckleberries provide a dense living carpet amongst the trees in this tranquil garden in northwestern America. *The Moss Garden, Bloedel Reserve, Bainbridge Island, WA, USA. Design: Owners, Prentice and Virginia Bloedel*

197

PAGE LEFT
TOP: Drift planting of *Stipa tenuissima* (feather grass) blends the view from this swimming pool to the hills beyond. *Napa, CA, USA. Design: Topher Delaney*

MIDDLE: Boulders are used here to blend the transition from patio garden to seashore in this Californian coastal garden. *Santa Barbara, CA, USA. Design: Isabelle Greene*

BOTTOM: This sweeping lawn gently harmonizes with the rolling hills of the landscape. *Somerset, England. Design: Owners, Octavian and Annabel von Hofmannsthal; James Alexander-Sinclair*

THIS PAGE
ABOVE: Wooden loungers lie amidst a bed of edible plants including herbs and salad crops. *"Lazy Salad Days" Garden, RHS Chelsea Flower Show 2003. Design: Paul Martin*

BELOW LEFT: A hammock is strung beneath the trees in this lush coastal woodland garden. *Seattle, WA, USA. Design: Owners, Lynn and Ralph Davis*

BELOW RIGHT: A metal geodesic pod seat is suspended above stratified concrete walls and paving. Succulents planted in the cracks include *Crassula ovata, Ceratonia siliqua, Cycas revoluta, Dracaena marginata, Echinocactus grusonii, Aloe mitriformis,* and *Aloe arborescens. "600 Days with Bradstone", RHS Chelsea Flower Show 2007. Design: Sarah Eberle*

TOP: Multi-coloured trampoline nets provide fun and exercise for children and adults alike here in this public park. *Showa Kinen Park, Tokyo, Japan. Design: Fumiaki Takano*

ABOVE LEFT: These undulating mound shapes use different-coloured recycled materials to provide a safe environment for children to enjoy. *"Safe Zone", International Garden Festival, Jardin de Metis, Quebec, Canada. Design: Stoss Landscape Urbanism*

ABOVE RIGHT: This organic-themed garden aims to encourage kids to go outside and play. The spiral stone pathway leads to a tunnel through a mound planted with meadow grass and the pretty succulent *Sempervivum tectorum*. *"The Marshalls Garden That Kids Really Want", RHS Chelsea Flower Show 2008. Design: Ian Dexter*

RIGHT TOP: Steps leading to this public park provide patterned and mosaic paving for running and playing through. Also featured are an ornamental fantasy clock and sturdy seating to either relax or jump over. *Showa Kinen Park, Tokyo, Japan. Design: Fumiaki Takano*

RIGHT: These small marble features propel grape-sized spurts of water into the air creating gentle surprises for small children dabbling in the water. *The Helen and Peter Bing Children's Garden, Huntington Botanic Gardens, CA, USA. Design: Huntington Botanic Gardens*

TOP LEFT: A snake created from turf mound shapes with mirrored glass balls for eyes appears amongst meadow planting. *"Snakes & Ladders", Gardening Scotland, Scotland. Design: Carole Gallagher-McCulloch*

TOP MIDDLE: The mosaic-tiled mouth of this ferocious creature creates a sand pit for brave children to play in. *Showa Kinen Park, Tokyo. Design: Fumiaki Takano*

TOP RIGHT: This stone snakeshead sculpture with enormous fangs lurks amongst soft-textured plants, including *Stipa tenuissima*, *Heuchera* 'Beauty Colour', *Stachys byzantina*, angelica, and *Pseudopanax crassiflora*. *"The Marshalls Garden That Kids Really Want", RHS Chelsea Flower Show 2008. Design: Ian Dexter*

LEFT: Umbrella-like water shapes, designed to be pierced and reshaped by small hands. *"The Vortex and Water Bells", The Helen and Peter Bing Children's Garden, Huntington Botanic Gardens, CA, USA. Design: Huntington Botanic Gardens*

ABOVE: This thatched children's playhouse with drawbridge entrance is bordered with flowering perennial plants edged with thick rope. *Flights of Fantasy Tudor House, RHS Chelsea Flower Show 2008. Design: Flights of Fantasy*

RIGHT: Children's footprints in the concrete path create intrigue to the entrance to this garden through a metal pergola. *The Helen and Peter Bing Children's Garden, Huntington Botanic Gardens, San Marino, CA, USA. Design: Huntington Botanic Gardens*

BELOW LEFT: Bricks are cleverly laid in a circular pattern to create this design for a productive vegetable garden. *Lincolnshire, England. Design: Paul Thompson and Ann-Marie Powell*

BOTTOM LEFT: Large red cabbages are grown here with perennial flowers and grasses to give unexpected drama to borders. *Cambo Walled Garden, Fife, Scotland. Design: Owner, Lady Catherine Erskine and head gardener, Elliot Forsyth*

RIGHT: In this Renaissance garden, buxus-edged squares of vegetables are planted for their colour as well as taste to create patterns and are interplanted with tree roses. *The Kitchen Garden, Château de Villandry, Indre-et-Loire, France*

BOTTOM RIGHT A combination of vegetables and flowers grow neatly in this compact plot by the edge of a Scottish loch. *Ardentinny, Argyllshire, Scotland. Design: Owners, Barry and Freda Waldapfel*

TOP: A rope-styled buxus hedge forms the centrepiece to this herb garden surrounded by *Digitalis purpurea* (foxglove). Herbs include *Armoracia rusticana*, syn. *Cochlearia armoracia* (horseradish), *Lavandula* (lavender), and *Onopordum acanthium* (cotton thistle). *Bridge Trust Gardens, Long Island, NY, USA. Design: Owners, Jim Kilpatric and Harry Neyens.*

ABOVE: A vast and ornamental productive garden with many herbs grown for consumption in an acclaimed restaurant. Enclosed by evergreen hedges of *Buxus sempervirens* and *Fagus sylvatica* (beech) are *Santolina chamaecyparissus*, and *Ruta graveolens* (rue). *The former Hotel Scholteshof, Limburg, Belgium. Design: Andre Steegmans for owner Roger Souvereyns*

LEFT: This generous herbaceous border grows against the warmth of the stone wall. Plants include *Crambe cordifolia*, *Nepeta* (catmint), and *Salvia officinalis* 'Purpurascens' (purple sage). *Dalemain House and Gardens, Penrith, Cumbria, England. Design: Owners, the Hasell family*

PREVIOUS PAGE

TOP: Space is given to the temporary seasonal colour of tulips by using containers in this herb garden. Enclosed by buxus hedging are mounds of *Rosmarinus officinalis* (rosemary), *Lavandula stoechas* (French lavender), *Salvia officinalis* 'Purpurascens' (purple sage), and *Origanum* (oregano). *Roscullen, Edinburgh, Scotland. Design: Owner, Mrs. Anne Duncan*

BOTTOM LEFT: Tree roses are planted in this checkerboard design using gravel between the squares and box hedging around the outside. Under planting consists of alliums, thyme, and mint. *Hill Barn House, Wiltshire, England. Design: Lanning Roper*

BOTTOM RIGHT: A mulberry tree is the centrepiece of this Tuscan herb garden. Tiled paths diagonally divide the raised beds which include *Artemisia absinthium, Mentha spicata, Lavandula stoechas, Borago officinalis* (borage), and *Alchemilla mollis. Borgo Santo Pietro, Chiusdino, Italy. Design: Helle Valsted and Christina Savage*

PAGE LEFT

TOP LEFT: This tiny herb garden shows just what can be grown in a small space. *"Feast of Herbs" Garden for the Herb Society, RHS Chelsea Flower Show 2003. Design: Cheryl Waller*

TOP RIGHT: This famous Scottish walled garden has long stone paths flanked with *Lavandula* (lavender), *Nepeta* (catmint), and geranium. Climbing the trellis are roses, *Lonicera* (honeysuckle), and clematis. *Crathes Castle (NTS), Aberdeenshire, Scotland. Design: Sir James Burnett of Leys*

LEFT: A raised herb bed provides the setting for a river of different varieties of creeping thyme flanked to the right by *Rosa mundi* (Gallica rose) and left *Salvia officinalis* 'Purpurascens' (purple sage). *Hollington Herb Garden, Berkshire, England. Design: Owners, Simon and Judith Hopkinson*

RIGHT: This collection of herbs and edible plants is displayed on the paved steps of this garden. All the herbs are kept in pots so they can be moved easily. They include *Ficus carica* (fig), *Lavandula stoechas* (French lavender), parsley, sage, rosemary, bay, chives, oregano, and *Echinacea* (coneflower). *The Herb Nursery, Rutland, England. Design: Owners Nancy, Peter and Christine Bench*

Galvanized metal rubbish bins are used here as containers for vegetable growing. Brassicas with a variety of textures are featured including *Cavolo nero* (Tuscan kale). *The Dillon Garden, Dublin, Ireland. Design: Owner, Helen Dillon*

Concrete troughs are versatile garden containers, used here for herbs and also as a small pond. Strawberries are also grown in a pot in the foreground. *WXD Cafe, London, England. Design: Dan Pearson and Steve Bradley*

This painted oak half barrel is planted with common thyme, applemint, rosemary, and common mint. *Alton Albany Farm, Barr, Ayrshire, Scotland. Design: Alasdair Currie, Tipple Containers*

STYLE

COUNTRY
COTTAGE
MEADOW
PRAIRIE
GRASS
FORMAL
GEOMETRIC
LANDSCAPED
MODERNIST
CONTEMPORARY
MINIMAL
ORIENTAL
GRAVEL
DRY
WATER
WOODED
EVERGREEN
EXOTIC
MEDITERRANEAN
RECYCLED
NIGHT
ROSE
ARCHITECTURAL PLANTS

Throughout history garden styles have evolved. Culture and fashion have influenced design just as much as they have changed every other medium. Today, as with our tastes in clothes, we are no longer limited to just one style as we would have been in previous centuries. We have a myriad "looks" from which to choose.

Having photographed so many different garden styles, I find that when I am trying to create my own space ideas pop in and out of my head like a pinball machine. Sometimes the range of choice leaves me breathless. Deciding and sticking to a plan can be the hardest part.

Probably the first consideration has to be the location and the established environment of the space. Whether you are in a desert situation or a lush woodland area the climate will largely dictate the type of style you decide upon. Of course it is possible to introduce vast oases to dry areas and to drain damp spots, but in most cases it makes more sense to work with the elements rather than against them. Function is also an important factor, as is budget: what will give most pleasure from the garden and how it will be used.

In my view, a garden should appeal to all the senses and a strong design style that makes use of all elements will help this. There is no point in having a lush garden with no sense of form. Neither is there sense in having a garden brilliantly landscaped, but with no attention to plants or the way the owner wishes to enjoy it. The garden needs both form and function to be successful. So the way you shape the space available should be the first consideration; the next should be the arrangement of the elements within it to your taste. You know when you are in a garden that works – everywhere you look, the composition is right and the elements fit together like the pieces of a jigsaw.

The history of garden design spans at least 4,000 years of human civilization so there is no shortage of patterns from which to choose. We know from Egyptian tomb paintings that ornamental gardens were taking shape as far back as the 1500 BC. Since then Persian, Greek, Chinese, Japanese, and Italian influences amongst others have made their mark.

More recently the English Garden has created a much-copied fashion. The "Lutyens–Jekyll" garden overflowed with hardy shrubs and herbaceous plants within an architectural structure of pergolas, stairs, and balustraded terraces. This combination of formal and informal – stone paths softened by voluptuous herbaceous borders heaving with lilies, lavender, delphiniums, and lupins – was in direct contrast to the very formal bedding schemes favoured by the previous generation in the 19th century. The new "natural" style was to define the "English garden" until modern times. In the last two decades the "new perennials" style, or "prairie planting", has made a big impact and inspired many of today's great garden designers, such as Piet Oudolf (page 228). His style now known as the "Dutch Wave" - a style of planting based on ecology, habitat planting, and perennials - was originally inspired by German nurseryman, plant breeder, and writer, Karl Foerster (1874-1940).

In the United States, Oehme, van Sweden & Associates' approach to landscape architecture, known as the "New American Garden" style, reflects the year-round beauty of the natural landscape (page 278). It frees plants from artificial forms and allows them to seek a natural course as they weave a tapestry across the entire garden plane. This is an alternative to the typical American garden, more relaxed and more sympathetic to the environment. Plants chosen for the New American Garden, especially perennials and ornamental grasses, require less maintenance, no deadheading or pesticides, and only limited water and fertilizer. The "hardscape" elements are carefully designed walls, terraces, and steps that complement the surrounding "softscape". When entering a garden, the visitor's attention is drawn first to dramatic spectacles of planting and then to the practical beauty of the built elements.

To quote James van Sweden himself: "Do gardens have to be so tame, so harnessed, so unfree? What's new about our New American Garden is what's new about America itself: it is vigorous and audacious, and it vividly blends the natural and the cultivated."

In this modern age of global communications many of us are in the fortunate position of being able to pick and mix from the very latest ideas and to borrow from different cultures and historic styles. In my opinion using these ideas and styles so that they work effortlessly in the space available is the true art of garden design.

RIGHT: Provence, France.
Design: Owner, Alex Dingwall-Main

ABOVE: *Alchemilla mollis* (lady's mantle) fizzes through the paving in this enclosed country courtyard. The stone walls support *Hydrangea anomala* subsp. *petiolaris* (climbing hydrangea), variegated ivy, clematis, *Jasminum* (jasmine), and *Lavandula* (lavender). Around the stone trough is *Geranium psilostemon*, *Zantedeschia* (calla lily), tree peony, astilbe, and ferns. *Hampshire, England. Design: Owner, Mrs. J. Budden*

RIGHT TOP: In this country garden a circular flowerbed features *Stachys* (lambs' ears) dotted with *Hemerocallis* (daylily). The backdrop is made of distinctive *Taxus baccata* (yew) topiary hedging. *Hummelo, Holland. Design: Owner, Piet Oudolf*

RIGHT MIDDLE: This circular pond forms the main focus of this formally laid out sunken garden. *Alchemilla mollis* has been allowed to grow around the base and thyme through the paving stones to soften the look. Buxus hedging encloses borders of flowering plants, including the airy mauve dots of *Verbena bonariensis*. *Holywell Hall, Lincolnshire, England. Design: Bunny Guinness*

RIGHT BOTTOM: A scented garden designed around the central *Pyrus salicifolia* 'Pendula' (weeping pear), under planted with *Hosta* 'Royal Standard'. *Jasmine officinale* and *Lonicera periclymenum* (honeysuckle) romp over a wooden pergola, whilst lavender and oriental lilies provide the perfume. *Norfolk Lavender Farm, Norfolk, England*

LEFT: An archway covered in honeysuckle leads the eye to an urn on a plinth filled with heuchera, enclosed by herbaceous borders and a lawn. *Bourne, Lincolnshire, England. Design: Owners, Ivan and Sadie Hall*

BELOW: Here an old farm courtyard has been completely transformed into a lush country garden. Varying levels add extra interest to the lawns and herbaceous borders. *Towcester, Northamptonshire, England. Design: Owner, James Alexander-Sinclair*

BOTTOM: This farmyard has been converted into a gravel garden. *Verbena bonariensis* and miscanthus are among the plants around the pool that give colour and texture to this area in late summer. *Somerset, England. Design: James Alexander-Sinclair*

ABOVE RIGHT: Hedges, shrubs, and trees give shelter to this neatly planted country garden. An eating area on a tiled patio looks onto the formal topiary garden and beyond are wilder areas of beautiful planting combinations. Plants include *Pyrus salicifolia* 'Pendula' (weeping pear), *Buxus sempervirens* hedging, *Taxus baccata* (yew), and *Fagus sylvatica* 'Purpurea Pendula' (weeping purple beech). *Hampshire, England. Design: Owner, Mrs. J. Budden*

RIGHT: The raised borders of this cottage garden are staged like a theatre so everything can be seen. They are filled with perennial plants, shrubs, and ornamental trees. Hostas including *Hosta* 'June' are grown in metal containers around the edge of the paved area. The tiny lawn is decorated with paving stones and buxus topiary. *Bourne, Lincolnshire, England. Design: Owners, Ivan and Sadie Hall*

PAGE LEFT

TOP: A paved patio is surrounded by full borders and flowering climbers in this cottage garden. The herbaceous perennial border includes geranium, nepeta, allium, aisyrinchium, roses, *Papaver somniferum*, *Centranthus ruber*, and *Onopordum acanthium*. *Northamptonshire, England. Design: James Alexander-Sinclair*

LEFT: This rural English cottage garden is planted with a mix of perennials and wild flowers. The drystone walls and rustic wood fencing lead the eye past the wheelbarrow with manure for spreading on beds to an old tractor in the shed. *The West Midlands-Shizuoka Goodwill Garden, RHS Chelsea Flower Show 2002. Design: Julian Dowle and Chris Caligari*

ABOVE: An expansive velvety green lawn leads to a country house surrounded by mature shrub borders and trees. *Shropshire, England. Design: Jenny Goodrich*

RIGHT: This country cottage border is planted with a mix of shrubs featuring hydrangea, *Rosmarinus officinalis* (rosemary), euphorbia, and *Buxus sempervirens*. In the foreground a large ball-shaped *Lonicera nitida* stands guard at the gateway. *Spalding, Lincolnshire, England. Design: Owners, Freddie Honnor and Maria Stamp*

LEFT: *Leucanthemum vulgare* (ox-eye daisies) feature in this country cottage garden blending the front area with the landscape beyond. Closer to the house buddleja flanks the front porch, while *Papaver orientale* (oriental poppies) and sedum add colour and texture to the border on each side. *Buckinghamshire, England. Design: Steve Bradley and Dan Pearson*

BELOW: A wooden gate in a *Fagus sylvatica* (beech) hedge opens into a pretty cottage garden planted with pink-flowering perennials, astrantia, and geranium. *Wiltshire, England. Design: Owner, Victoria Kerr*

RIGHT: A border filled to brimming with *Geranium psilostemon* contrasts here with the yellow flowers in this front lawn "mini-meadow", reflecting the yellow-painted front door and golden hops climbing beside it. In the background the view of Loch Long fades into the distance. *Ardentinny, Argyllshire, Scotland. Design: Owners, Barry and Freda Waldapfel*

223

LEFT TOP: Here a path has been mown through a long meadow of *Knautia arvensis* flanked by *Crataegus* (hawthorn) trees. *Scampston Hall, Malton, North Yorkshire, England. Design: Owners, Sir Charles and Lady Legard*

FAR LEFT: A sweeping countryside view, including an orchard with contrasting mown and long meadow grass. *Hertfordshire, England. Design: Owner, Kim Wilde*

LEFT: A manicured ziggurat of mown grass rises above a meadow planted with *Knautia arvensis*, grasses, and *Prunus* x *yedoensis* (cherry) trees. *The Walled Garden, Scampston Hall, Malton, North Yorkshire, England. Design: Piet Oudolf*

ABOVE: In this garden, the designers have deliberately encouraged a wild meadow as a link between the highly cultivated and the natural. *Irvington, NY, USA. Design: Reed Hilderbrand*

ABOVE: A natural driftwood tree stumpery is the focus of this mixed meadow garden. Flowers include *Papaver rhoeas* (corn poppy), *Eschscholzia californica* (California poppy), and *Centaurea cyanus* (cornflower). *The Natural Driftwood Sculpture Garden, Hampton Court Show 2001, England. Design: Marney Hall*

ABOVE RIGHT: This meadow is enclosed by natural woodland and divided by mown paths for access. *West Stockbridge, MA, USA. Design: Reed Hilderbrand*

RIGHT: A swathe of natural meadow planting provides a gentle contrast to a mown lawn and mature deciduous trees. *Long Island, NY, USA. Design: Reed Hilderbrand*

LEFT: *Centaurea cyanus* (cornflower), *Agrostemma githago* (corn cockle), and *Chamaemelum nobile* are used to create a mini-meadow in this small garden. *Ardentinny, Argyllshire, Scotland. Design: Owners, Barry and Freda Waldapfel*

LEFT: A variety of textured perennial plants and grasses are designed as prairie planting in this garden space in Millenium Park. *Lurie Garden, Chicago, IL, USA. Planting design: Piet Oudolf. Landscape design: Kathryn Gustafson*

BELOW: A hedge of rosemary divides this garden into areas of contrasting textures, form, and colour. Textural grasses, *Stipa tenuissima*, are interplanted with the sculptural agaves and highlighted with *Eschscholzia californica* (California poppy). A grove of olive trees provides shade and a sculptural sphere by Grace Knowlton provides dramatic effect. *"The Garden of Contrasts", Cornerstone Festival of Gardens, Sonoma, CA, USA. Design: James van Sweden and Sheila Brady*

LEFT: A gravel path divides these full and dramatic borders of perennial flowers and grasses. Included in the mix are asters, *Persicaria amplexicaulis*, *Eupatorium purpureum*, *Sedum* 'Herbstfreude', *Sedum* 'Matrone', *Calamagrostis* x *acutiflora* 'Karl Foerster', and *Miscanthus sinensis* cultivars. *The Double Prairie Borders, Cambo Walled Garden, Kingsbarns, Fife, Scotland. Design: Owner, Lady Catherine Erskine and head gardener, Elliot Forsyth*

MIDDLE LEFT: Grasses grown in rows for their seed are naturally ornamental. *Emory Knoll Farms, Maryland, USA. Design: Ed and Lucie L. Snodgrass*

BOTTOM LEFT: Ornamental grass border catches the light at the end of the day — *Panicum virgatum* (switchgrass) and *Saccharum contortum* (bent-awn plumegrass) with *Panicum amarum* 'Dewy Blue' in the background. *Landenberg, PA, USA. Design: Owners, Rick Darke and Melinda Zoehrer*

BELOW: A narrow boardwalk leads to a secluded seating area in this suburban back garden planted as a prairie. It is full of *Rudbeckia* (black-eyed Susan) and *Echinacea* (coneflower). *Sheffield, South Yorkshire, England. Design: Owner, Professor James Hitchmough*

FOLLOWING PAGE
TOP:
This contemporary visitors centre is set amongst drifts of flowering herbaceous perennial plants and grasses. *Mount Stuart, Isle of Bute, Scotland. Garden design: James Alexander-Sinclair*

BOTTOM:
Drifts of *Stipa tenuissima* blend the garden area around this swimming pool into the landscape beyond. *Napa, CA, USA. Design: Topher Delaney*

ABOVE: This exposed coastal garden has a large border of ornamental grasses which sweep around the lawn in an arc exposing magnificent views over the area. *San Francisco Bay Area, CA, USA. Design: Topher Delaney*

FAR LEFT: Here disused railroad tracks are planted with ornamental grass, trees, and shrubs so they look good throughout the year. *Viburnum x bodnantense* 'Dawn' is planted in a rhythm down the line. *Gansevoort Woodland & Grassland, The High Line, New York, NY, USA. Planting design: Piet Oudolf*

LEFT: Prairie planting of native North American *Andropogon scoparius* (little blue stem) with asters are used in this experimental town garden so there is little need for watering. *"One Drop at a Time", Elmhurst, IL, USA. Design: Marcus de la Fleur*

231

ABOVE: Grasses and other leafy
perennials such as *Euphorbia griffithii*
'Dixter' (spurge), rodgersia, and
ornamental grasses surround a circular
dish-style pond. Leading the eye away
from this feature are *Buxus
sempervirens* squares with stainless
steel water features. *"Evolution", The
Gardens Illustrated Garden, RHS Chelsea
Flower Show 2000. Design: Arne
Maynard and Piet Oudolf*

LEFT: Garden mounds of tall grasses
allude to the landscape of the Gaspé
region of Canada (rye, barley, oats, and
triticale). The posts are translucent core
samples and contain a range of textures
collected from the region. *"Core Sample",
International Garden Festival, Jardin de
Metis/Reford Gardens, Quebec, Canada.
Design: Pete and Alissa North*

RIGHT: Vibrant red-stemmed *Cornus* (dogwood), ornamental grasses, and trees in autumn colour surround and are reflected in a lake. *Lady Farm, Somerset, England. Design: Owner, Judy Pearce*

BELOW: White gravel is used to make a path through large ornamental grass borders, with *Miscanthus sinensis*, gaura, and *Rosa* 'Iceberg'. *"The White Work", Le Jardin de l'Alchimiste, Eygalieres en Provence, France. Design: Eric Ossart and Arnaud Maurieres*

BOTTOM: The expanse of lawn is graduated into the garden area here by drifts of herbaceous perennials such as *Perovskia* (Russian sage) and ornamental grasses. *Salem, NY, USA. Design: Oehme, van Sweden*

ABOVE: In this garden swathes of
molinia run through the close mown
grass of the lawn. *The Walled Garden,
Scampston Hall, North Yorkshire,
England. Design: Piet Oudolf*

ABOVE: A water channel leading to the entrance of a glass conservatory is the main feature of this formal garden. Either side it is flanked by a neatly clipped buxus hedge parterre with decorative spirals. *Lancaster, Lancashire, England. Design: David Redmore*

RIGHT ABOVE: A pleached hornbeam allée draws the eye to the sculpture at the end. A small rill and buxus balls in zinc containers help to emphasize the direction. *Bourne, Lincolnshire, England. Design: Owners, Ivan and Sadie Hall*

RIGHT: This formal sunken garden with stone paths and water feature is planted with brightly coloured annuals to emphasize the length of the stripey lawn. Parallel borders include heliotrope and pelargonium. *The Pool Garden, Hampton Court Palace Gardens, Surrey, England*

ABOVE: A mix of low geometric shapes in *Buxus sempervirens* and taller *Taxus baccata* (yew) sculptural topiary form this historic topiary garden dating from 1694. *Levens Hall, Kendal, Cumbria, England*

LEFT TOP: This sunken garden is divided with geometric precision. The pergola at the far end gives transparency for the view of the distant landscape. *The Edwardian Formal Garden, Hestercombe Gardens, Somerset, England. Design: Sir Edwin Lutyens and Gertrude Jekyll*

LEFT MIDDLE: Geometric beds are edged with buxus hedging in this formal kitchen garden. Repeat planting of bright red *Crocosmia* 'Lucifer' emphasizes the outer spaces. The Victorian-style glasshouse in the background houses exotic plants. *Mount Stuart, Isle of Bute, Scotland. Redesign: Rosemary Verey; cutting garden borders: James Alexander-Sinclair*

LEFT BOTTOM: This area of garden is dominated by the water channel flanked by topiary yew cones. Patterns and shapes are defined by an avenue of deciduous trees and beds of colourful spring bulbs. *Keukenhof, Holland. Design: J. D. and L. P. Zocher*

BELOW: These linear terraced gardens are defined by evergreen hedging and limestone walls. Irregular steps lead to the central fountain. *Jardin à la Française, Le Mas de la Brune, Eygalieres en Provence, France.*

BOTTOM: A Saxon moat encloses this formal topiary garden with *Taxus baccata* (yew) topiary and *Buxus sempervirens* hedging. Mature deciduous trees shelter the area, but a wide track is left open to allow a view of the landscape beyond. *Great Fosters Hotel, Egham, Surrey, England. Design: W. H. Romaine-Walker and Gilbert Jenkins; recent renovations: Kim Wilkie*

ABOVE: Frothy white flowers feature in the borders of this otherwise structural geometric green garden with *Buxus sempervirens* balls amongst the stone shapes. *"The Woolworths Garden", RHS Chelsea Flower Show 2004. Design: The Pickard School of Gardening*

ABOVE LEFT: This neat, geometric brick and stone paved patio sits amongst borders of flowering shrubs in a townhouse courtyard garden. *Georgetown, Washington, DC, USA. Design: Oehme, van Sweden*

LEFT: A checkerboard of granite squares makes a perfect platform for these terracotta containers filled with cones of *Buxus microphylla x antzam 'Antarctica'. New York Botanical Garden, Bronx, NY, USA. Design: New York Botanical Garden*

ABOVE RIGHT: A spiral labyrinth of buxus forms the centrepiece of the composition while pruned bay trees form a grid over the garden to "illustrate the timeless quality of Le Nôtre's style". *"Homage to Le Nôtre", RHS Chelsea Flower Show 2000. Design: Tom Stuart-Smith*

RIGHT: Geometric patterns of buxus hedging keep a tight edge around lines of vegetables punctuated with standard roses and fruit trees. *Château de Villandry, Indre-et-Loire, France. Design: Historic; recent rennovations: Joachim Carvallo*

FAR RIGHT: This labyrinth design is cut into meadow grass revealing the soil beneath. *Dumfries and Galloway, Scotland. Design: Jim Buchanan*

LEFT TOP: This terraced lawn is gently landscaped into curves and slopes. Trees have been planted for structure, including sorbus, pine, and *Acer pseudoplatanus* (sycamore maple). *Cornwall, England. Design: David Buurma*

LEFT BELOW: Precise grading and masonry create the armature for flexible garden plots among the terraces of this award-winning shrub and vine area of an arboretum. *M. Victor and Frances Leventritt Garden, The Arnold Arboretum of Harvard University, Boston, MA, USA. Design: Reed Hilderbrand*

RIGHT: Inlaid stone steps help define the graduated slope of this lawn. *Irvington, NY, USA. Design: Reed Hilderbrand*

BELOW: This sculpted earth and turf amphitheatre makes a dramatic end to an avenue of trees and screens out the sights and sounds of cars from a nearby motorway. *Great Fosters Hotel, Egham, Surrey, England. Design: Kim Wilkie*

ABOVE: This sweeping mound uses the water to create a French curve, which is composed of different curves. The curves extend from the snail-hook (right) to the causeway (centre), then to the snake mound (left). *The Garden of Cosmic Speculation, Dumfries and Galloway, Scotland. Design: Owners, Charles Jencks and Maggie Keswick*

LEFT: The geometric lines of a small formal rose garden reflect the architecture of the iconic modernist residence behind. *The Donnell Garden, Sonoma County, CA, USA. Design: Thomas Church, with Lawrence Halprin and George Rockrise*

LEFT BELOW: This wooden deck striped with grey-coloured concrete continues up to the house via wooden steps. Along the edge of the walls planting includes bamboo and *Zantedeschia* (calla lily). *Bay Area, San Francisco, CA, USA. Design: Topher Delaney*

RIGHT: The centrepiece of this spacious gravel courtyard is an *Acer griseum* tree planted in a square bed with rusted steel edge. A burbling fountain trickles into a simple dish-like form in the background. *Orinda, CA, USA. Design: Topher Delaney*

BELOW: Stripes of moss accentuate the perspective of this driveway leading to the main courtyard garden. On the right a citrus tree is planted in a concrete urn amongst libertia and *Phormium* (New Zealand flax). On the left a *Tamarix* (tamarisk) overhangs a bed of *Festuca glauca* (blue fescue). *Orinda, CA, USA. Design: Topher Delaney*

FAR LEFT: A deck projects above a layer of shrubs into the garden from this modernist house in the English countryside. *Millstream Sculpture Garden, Wiltshire, England. Design: Owner, Michael Newberry*

LEFT: A simple mass planting of ivy covers the ground within the rectangular raised beds outside this iconic single storey modernist house. Photographed 1/08/2008. *Indianapolis Museum of Art, Miller House and Garden in Columbus, IN, USA. Garden design: Dan Urban Kiley. Miller House design: Eero Saarinen*

ABOVE: An infinity swimming pool dominates this lawn with water falling over the edge of the stonework in the direction of the Hudson River. *Irvington, NY, USA. Design: Reed Hilderbrand*

ABOVE: Contemporary outdoor living space with kitchen, surrounded by a wooden decked seating area and sub-tropical planting. *Trailfinders Australian Garden, RHS Chelsea Flower Show 2010. Design: Scott Wynd*

LEFT: Sounds of children talking emanate from this enigmatic reflective box that rises out of a fallow field in this installation garden. *"A boîte noire", International Garden Festival, Jardin de Metis/Reford Gardens, Quebec, Canada. Design: Jasmine Corbeil and Stephane Bertrand with Jean-Maxime Dufresne*

RIGHT ABOVE: Curvy blue seating, carpets, and walls feature in this contemporary roof garden. *San Francisco, CA, USA. Design: Topher Delaney*

RIGHT MIDDLE: Mexican immigrant workers are honoured in this garden. Three symbolic walls divide the space – rusty metal (United States–Mexican border), red-painted plywood (the dead), and stones seeping water (tears). *"Small Tribute to Immigrant Workers", Cornerstone Festival of Gardens, Sonoma, CA, USA. Design: Mario Schjetnan*

RIGHT: In this contemporary garden glass pyramids containing solar panels stand in borders of herbaceous perennials. A studio is built into the hillside supported by gabion walls, and recycled scaffolding boards are used for the screen walls. *The Marshalls' Sustainability Garden, RHS Chelsea Flower Show 2007. Design: Scenic Blue Design Team*

ABOVE: This contemporary pergola with bench beneath acts as the framework for a display of climbing roses. Colourful borders below include alliums, tulips, *Foeniculum vulgare* (fennel), *Dianthus* (pink), *Rosmarinus officinalis* (rosemary), and santolina. *"The Walled Garden", RHS Chelsea Flower Show 2003. Design: Judith Wise and Juliet McKelvey*

ABOVE LEFT: Limestone terrace garden with seat and reflecting pool, surrounded by lawns and rendered wall with sculptures by Stephen Cox, large perennial borders, and a geometric grid of standard trees. At one end is a polished stainless steel water feature. Planting includes *Carpinus betulus* (hornbeam), *Verbascum* 'Suttons Apricot', *Tulipa* 'Orange Princess', *Stipa gigantea*, and *Santolina chamaecyparissus*. *The Sanctuary Garden, RHS Chelsea Flower Show 2002. Design: Stephen Woodhams*

LEFT: Against a vertical background of large vine leaves is a simple border of repeat-flowering perennials including alliums and roses. *The Hidden Gardens, Glasgow, Scotland. Design: nva organisation and City Design Cooperative*

RIGHT ABOVE: Freestanding wooden screens painted in traditional Swedish red iron oxide paint provide the backdrop here for a garden of subtlety. Layers of green foliage and white flowers cleanly butt together. At ground level *Asarum europaeum* and *Fritillaria meleagris* var. *unicolor* subvar. *alba*. Then *Matteuccia struthiopteris*, *Hosta* 'Patriot' (plantain lily), *Digitalis* 'Saltwood Summer', and *Iris sibirica* 'White Swirl'. In the middle sits *Viburnum opulus* 'Roseum' and finally at top level Betula *utilis* var. *jacquemontii* 'Doorenbos' and flat-crowned *Malus* 'Evereste'. *A Tribute to Linnaeus, RHS Chelsea Flower Show 2007. Design: Ulf Nordfjell*

RIGHT BELOW: A waterfall cascades over irregular jagged stones providing a backdrop for a planting of many shades and textures of green. Hosta, ferns, *Vinca* (periwinkle), iris, and clematis are overhung by *Salix* (willow) foliage. *"Pavilion of Blue Waves", Jardin Atlantique, Gare Montparnasse, Paris, France. Design: Brun, Penna, and Schnitzler*

ABOVE: Bold, colourful planting amongst *Stipa gigantea* of iris, poppies, verbascum, and alliums make up the foreground to this display garden which features a William Pye polished stainless steel and clear acrylic polymer water feature. *Olea europaea* (olive) trees are planted in the islands amongst the shallow pools. *"A Garden For All Time"*, *RHS Chelsea Flower Show 2000. Design: Arabella Lennox-Boyd*

ABOVE: A mixture of stone paving with sections of wooden boardwalk provide the paths on which to walk through this tranquil garden with water pools shaded by bamboo. Seclusion is further created by glass screens. *"In The Grove"*, for his late Highness Sheikh Zayed bin Sultan Al-Nahyan, RHS Chelsea Flower Show 2005. Design: Christopher Bradley-Hole

LEFT: A wooden boardwalk makes a path around this low-maintenance town garden using drought-tolerant and architectural plants in pebble beds. *London, England. Design: Matthew Vincent*

ABOVE RIGHT: Stone paving slabs form the path in this tiny town garden surrounded by pink-flowering *Persicaria bistorta. Angelica archangelica* provides an architectural element to the planting design. *The Marshalls Living Street, RHS Chelsea Flower Show 2009. Design: Ian Dexter*

ABOVE FAR RIGHT: Amid stone paving slabs a mass of small cubes of clipped *Buxus sempervirens* form the basis of this unusual long bed punctuated with tall white birches. *Parc André Citroën, Paris, France. Design: Gilles Clément, Patrick Berger, Alain Provost, Jean-Paul Viguier, Jean-François Jodry*

RIGHT: This minimalist garden is set in a leafy London square. Its unusual flat square lawns and pools are flanked by neatly clipped topiary hedges. *The Hempel Hotel, London, England. Design: Anouska Hempel*

ABOVE: The backbone of this enclosed
garden is a fence of oak slats in
quincuncial pattern inspired by early
Arabian gardens. *Carpinus betulus* and
Taxus baccata are clipped into verticals
to follow the theme. Planting in the
border includes *Stipa gigantea*, rose
varieties, *Knautia macedonica*, and
geranium. *Hortus Conclusus, for his
late Highness Sheikh Zayed bin Sultan
Al-Nahyan, RHS Chelsea Flower Show
2004. Design: Christopher Bradley-Hole*

TOP: A sea of raked gravel with grass islands is surrounded and complemented by clipped azaleas in flower and trees, including *Acer palmatum* var. *dissectum* (Japanese maple), *Pinus* (pine), and *Prunus* (cherry). *Portland Japanese Garden, Portland, OR, USA. Design: Professor Takuma Ton*

ABOVE: An oriental-style moss garden created using Japanese maple, ornamental grasses, ferns, azalea, and primula. Stones and rocks have been placed throughout the garden, several being used as a bench at the far side. *Portland, OR, USA. Design: Owners, Norm Kalbfleisch and Neil Matteucci*

RIGHT TOP: This Japanese Zen garden has been built at the water's edge with gravel raked meticulously around carefully placed boulders. Around the edge of this space grows *Ophiopogon planiscapus* 'Nigrescens' (Black lilyturf) and *Ophiopogon japonicus* (Mondo grass) ground cover. *Floriade 2002, Holland*

RIGHT MIDDLE: This raked gravel Zen garden has been created in a public park surrounded by woodland. The wooden boardwalk with hand rail winds slowly to a tea house. *Japanese Garden, Ronneby, Sweden. Design: Sven-Ingvar Andersson*

RIGHT BOTTOM: Here a roof in central London has been transformed into a contemporary-styled Zen-raked gravel garden using boulders, slates, shrubs, pine trees, Japanese maples, and stone paving. *Marylebone, London, England. Design: Tony Heywood*

ABOVE: This Moon Gate leads the way through to the entrance courtyard of a Chinese garden and frames the view of a flowering rhododendron. *Lan Su Chinese Garden, Portland, OR, USA. Design: Kuang Zhen Yan*

ABOVE RIGHT: Many stone steps lead up this hill lined by moss and guided by a delicate wooden fence and hand rail. Camellias are planted for their foliage and spring colour. *Portland Japanese Garden, Portland, OR, USA. Design: Professor Takuma Tono*

RIGHT TOP: The surface of this shallow water garden is broken only by slate rocks, a slim, twisting Burlington slate path, and water lilies. Planting seen here at the end of the garden is *Phyllostachys aurea, Phyllostachys sulphurea f. viridis* (bamboo), *Gunnera manicata, Pterocarya fraxinifolia,* and clipped *Taxus baccata* (yew) hedging. *The Daily Telegraph Garden, RHS Chelsea Flower Show 2008. Design: Arabella Lennox-Boyd*

RIGHT: This garden illustrates the many varieties and textures of bamboo. The low hedges are clipped bamboo whilst stands of giant bamboo provide shelter and height. *La Bambouseraie, Anduze, France. Design: Eugène Mazel and the Negre family*

FAR RIGHT: An oriental style is given to this American garden by stepping stones and neatly planted *Buxus sempervirens* and *Alchemilla mollis* (lady's mantle) positioned under a small tree. *Irvington, NY, USA. Design: Reed Hilderbrand*

ABOVE: The elements of stone and sand evoke meditative moods in this Zen garden as seen from the deck of a tea house. Geometric patterns of grass, stone paved squares, and undulating green mounds lead to the coniferous trees surrounding the garden that provide a contrasting dark backdrop. *Bloedel Reserve, WA, USA. Design: Professor Koichi Kawana*

LEFT: A gravel courtyard blends with the traditional pink colour of this old cottage. It is planted with greens and soft greys and given structure by *Laurus nobilis* trees, underplanted with *Ophiopogon planiscapus* 'Nigrescens', *Buxus sempervirens* balls and cones. *Shropshire, England. Design: Jenny Goodrich*

LEFT BELOW: This town front garden uses a simple gravel bed to display a carved wood sculpture by the artist Walter Bailey. *Brighton, Sussex, England. Design: Owners*

BELOW: Concrete paths weave amongst the slate beds which display stone sculptures, including *Core* (Cored Sculpture) 1978 (basalt, centre) and *End Pieces* 1974 (Swedish granite, left).

The former Isamu Noguchi Sculpture Museum, Long Island City, NY, USA. Design: Isamu Noguchi

RIGHT: A sweeping gravel driveway and turning circle make an impressive entrance to this contemporary residence. *Salem, NY, USA. Design: Oehme, van Sweden*

BOTTOM: A large cushion-like bed of thyme dominates this gravel driveway leading to the main house. Borders are filled with flowering azalea, ornamental trees including maple and *Corylus avellana* 'Contorta' (corkscrew hazel). *Portland, OR, USA. Design: Owners, Norm Kalbfleisch and Neil Matteucci*

ABOVE: Slate is used in this town garden both in chipping form as a mulch and as the base of fountains providing a cool contrast to the wooden fencing and trellis. *Buxus sempervirens* balls, *Alchemilla mollis* (lady's mantle), and ferns provide the main source of green-textured foliage. *Hackney, London, England. Design: Joe Swift and The Plant Room*

ABOVE RIGHT: Raised beds of hot-coloured gravel, painted fencing and poles were inspired by Aboriginal art from the Australian outback and evoke the idea of a dried-up creek. Drought-tolerant plants include *Eucalyptus pauciflora* subsp. *niphophila* (snow gum), *Ophiopogon planiscapus* 'Nigrescens', *Phormium* (New Zealand flax), sedum, and iris. *"Kelly's Creek", RHS Chelsea Flower Show 2002. Design: Alison Wear and Miranda Melville*

PAGE RIGHT

TOP LEFT: Cumbrian slates are used in this romantic garden, both as flagstones and to retain the wildflower bank. A narrow pathway leads out of the garden over a stile, while a living willow arbour provides a place to rest among the flowers, notably *Geranium pratense*, *Aquilegia vulgaris*, *Aquilegia* 'Nora Barlow', *Geranium sanguineum* var. *striatum*, *Geranium* 'Kashmir Pink', and *Persicaria bistorta* 'Superba'. *"The Cumbrian Fellside Garden", RHS Chelsea Flower Show 2005. Design: Kim Wilde and Richard Lucas. Slate spheres design: Andrew Loudon*

TOP RIGHT: Railway sleeper (railroad tie) steps lead down to a gravel path and stone paved patio with a raised pond in this garden full of architectural plants, featuring *Phormium* (New Zealand flax), *Trachelospermum jasminoides* (star jasmine) climber, *Pittosporum tobira*, *Miscanthus sinensis* 'Zebrinus', and *Trachycarpus fortunei* (chusan palm, windmill palm). *Kew, Surrey, England. Design: Matthew Vincent*

RIGHT: Classical columns nestle in the gravel and stone slab paths in this garden shaded by giant bamboo. *San Jose, CA, USA. Design: Owner, Cevan Forristt*

FAR RIGHT: Light gravel paths feature strongly in this garden contrasting with the coloured walls and metal planter containing *Libertia grandiflora*, while blending with the smooth stone bench. Around the perimeter are pleached *Carpinus betulus* (hornbeam) giving linear form to this contemporary-styled garden. *The Daily Telegraph Garden, RHS Chelsea Flower Show 2009. Design: Ulf Nordfjell*

ABOVE: An area of garden is made to represent the desert, using a dry terrain scattered with flint rocks and pebbles. Drought-tolerant planting includes *Eschscholzia californica*, dasylirion, agave, agapanthus, *Beschorneria yuccoides*, and echium. *East Ruston Old Vicarage, Norfolk, England. Design: Alan Gray and Graham Robeson*

ABOVE: The planting patterns in this Californian garden are devised to represent the local landscape as seen from the air. A wide variety of plants is used including roses, poppies, and many succulents. Agaves and figs climb the wall. *The former Valentine residence, Santa Barbara, CA, USA. Design: Isabelle Greene*

RIGHT: In this desert garden a circular seating area is made of coloured concrete. Rebar rods emerge from the surrounding walls, and the central fire pit has been made out of red lava rocks. The garden is planted with succulents and cacti native to the area. *Baja Valley Garden, Paradise Valley, AZ, USA. Design: Steve Martino*

ABOVE: This impressive drought-tolerant border includes a variety of agave, yucca, palms, and succulents. *The Ruth Bancroft Garden, Walnut Creek, CA, USA. Design: Owner, Ruth Bancroft*

RIGHT: An entrance garden path is flanked by mounded sand dunes and shaded by a variety of trees, shrubs, and ornamental grasses. On the right is *The Gateway Bell*, 2003, by Toshiko Takaezu. *"The Dunes", Longhouse Reserve, Long Island, NY, USA. Design: Jack Lenor-Larsen*

TOP LEFT: This clever swimming pool design gives an illusion of infinity and links the view to the Hudson River below. *Fargo Lane, Irvington, NY, USA. Design: Reed Hilderbrand*

FAR LEFT: A planting of native meadow flowers blends this garden swimming pool into its surrounding landscape. *Napa, CA, USA. Design: Topher Delaney*

LEFT: Starkly minimal, this stone canal water feature is enlivened by the pink flowers of a *Nymphaea* (waterlily). *Parc André Citroën, Paris, France. Design: Gilles Clément and Alain Provost*

ABOVE: Cutting through the heart of this gravel garden is a stylish shallow reflecting pool which appears to dissolve into the landscape beyond through a stone wall. *Tregony, Cornwall, England. Design: David Buurma*

RIGHT: A long fine rill flanked by criss-crossed willow screens draws the eye into the heart of this garden. *Le Jardin de l'Alchimiste, Eygalieres en Provence, France. Design: Eric Ossart and Arnaud Maurières*

TOP LEFT: The sound of water adds a tranquil dimension as a rill and waterfall empty into a pool. Large drifts of perennial plants and flowers soften the edges of the stonework. *Salem, NY, USA. Design: Oehme, van Sweden*

ABOVE LEFT: Solid paved stepping stones over this pond allow the path to continue unhindered through drifts of ornamental grasses. *Petersfield, Hampshire, England. Design: Acres Wild*

LEFT: A magnificent water channel flanked by distinctive flowering perennial borders. Typha feature in the pool in the foreground where the water falls, but otherwise the pool is kept clear to reflect the planting and sky. *The Dillon Garden, Dublin, Ireland. Design Owner, Helen Dillon*

ABOVE: A pool with bubbling fountain is the focus at the end of an avenue. The foliage of multi-coloured coleus is used to decorate the edges. Photographed 1/8/2008. *Indianapolis Museum of Art, Miller House and Garden, Columbus, IN, USA. Design: Daniel Urban Kiley*

RIGHT: An eco-friendly house looks out onto a meadow garden with a wooden bridge to a natural, wildlife-friendly pond. *Diss, Norfolk, England. Design: Paul Thompson and Ann-Marie Powell*

BELOW: This natural-looking pond in a woodland garden is full of marginal plants. *Carex pendula*, gunnera, and iris are planted to add texture, colour, and interest. *The former Heronswood Nursery, Bainsbridge Island, WA, USA. Design: Owners, Daniel J. Hinkley and Robert Jones*

LEFT TOP: Mature oak trees shade the path through this elegant woodland garden. *Santa Barbara, CA, USA. Design: Isabelle Greene*

LEFT MIDDLE: A simple path leads through a grove of white-barked *Betula jacquemontii* (Himalayan birch). *Bloedel Reserve, Bainbridge Island, WA, USA. Design: Owners, Prentice and Virginia Bloedel*

LEFT BOTTOM: Mature deciduous trees shed a carpet of autumn leaves in this gently sloping woodland garden. *Beaconsfield, Buckinghamshire, England. Design: Owners*

BELOW: A boardwalk leads through this woodland garden with damp-loving plants. *Camarthen, Wales. Design: Owners, Bob and Rannveig Wallis*

RIGHT: Decaying fallen tree trunks crisscross their way through a dense living carpet of moss, ferns, and native North American woodland plants. *The Moss Garden, Bloedel Reserve, Bainbridge Island, WA, USA. Design: Owners, Prentice and Virginia Bloedel*

BOTTOM: Cloud-pruned *Carpinus betulus* (hornbeam) take centrestage in this woodland garden. Many layers and textures of foliage plants froth with white flowers below. *Rodgersia podophylla*, asarum, peony, geranium, and epimedium contrast against a *Taxus baccata* (yew) hedge behind. *The Laurent-Perrier Garden, RHS Chelsea Flower Show 2008. Design: Tom Stuart-Smith*

TOP: *Ceanothus thyrsiflorus* var. *repens* (creeping blueblossom) creates a sea of blue below live oak trees. *Santa Barbara, CA, USA. Design: Isabelle Greene*

BOTTOM LEFT: These white-stemmed *Betula jacquemontii* (Himalayan birch) trees have been generously underplanted, notably with pastel-coloured flowering rhododendrons such as *Rhododendron* 'Lem's Monarch' to give light to this woodland garden. *Juntunen Farm and Gardens, Mount Vernon, WA, USA. Design: Owner, Mari Juntunen*

BOTTOM RIGHT: Trees in this apple orchard are underplanted with spring bulbs giving plenty of bright cheerful colour in the long meadow grass. Also giving colour are cowslips and bluebells. *Cumbria, England. Design: Owner, Ian Gregg*

RIGHT: An installation of 50 speakers with small wind-power generators are woven among a stand of poplar trees. Drifts of electronic sound are diffused as wind sensors react to changing weather conditions. An ongoing sonic conversation results. *"soundFIELD" International Garden Festival, Jardin de Metis/Reford Gardens, Quebec, Canada. Design: Douglas Moffat and Steve Bates*

RIGHT BELOW: These fruit-laden apple trees frame the view to large borders of perennial grasses and flowers in this inspirational walled garden. *Cambo Walled Garden, Fife, Scotland. Design: Owner, Lady Catherine Erskine and head gardener, Elliot Forsyth*

BOTTOM: A regiment of white-stemmed birch trees are planted in the lawn shading a stone sculpture by Emily Young. *Somerset, England. Design: Owners, Octavian and Annabel von Hofmannsthal*

LEFT: This evergreen "doughnut" shape of *Taxus baccata* gives year round interest to an island bed of shrubs and contrasts with the tone and texture of the *Buxus sempervirens*. *Carestown Steading, Deskford, Buckie, Moray and Nairn, Scotland. Design: Owner, Rora Paglieri*

RIGHT: *Eriobotrya japonica* (loquat tree) shades the gravel relaxing area below. Corten rusted steel sheets are used as edging for the raised bed with flowering perennials. *Orinda, CA, USA. Design: Topher Delaney*

FAR RIGHT: Subtle tones of green and textures of foliage provided by *Buxus sempervirens*, *Ilex crenata*, and *Taxus baccata* create a stage and backdrop for *Crataegus persimilis* trees. *Carestown Steading, Deskford, Buckie, Moray and Nairn, Scotland. Design: Owner, Rora Paglieri*

RIGHT: Containers are used in this area of an evergreen garden to enable plants to be moved as the seasons change. Planting includes: *Prunus laurocerasus* (cherry laurel), *Griselinia littoralis*, *Olea europaea* (olive), cupressus, choisya, gunnera shoots, *Laurus nobilis* (bay), acer, *Photinia* 'Red Robin', and flowering magnolia. *Twickenham, London, England. Design: Owner, Ian Sidaway*

FAR RIGHT: This neat little evergreen border features clipped *Lonicera nitida* and *Buxus sempervirens* topiary balls set against a backdrop of *Griselinia littoralis* and larger ball-shaped *Pittosporum tobira*. *Twickenham, London, England. Design: Owner, Ian Sidaway*

LEFT: Known as the "Abstract Wall" the granite slabs used for this wall and waterfall were recycled from demolished buildings in Rio de Janeiro. It is a perfect backdrop for epiphytes, while the pool provides a setting for aquatic and tropical plants including *Nelumbo nucifera* (sacred lotus). *Sítio Roberto Burle Marx, Rio de Janeiro, Brazil. Design: Roberto Burle Marx*

LEFT BELOW: This masterpiece of landscape design features an artful waterfall alongside a ceramic-tiled outbuilding. The curved lines of the design, spatial structure, and orange, yellow, and red colours are characteristic of the mature work of Burle Marx. *Fazenda Marambaia, formerly the Odette Monteiro Residence, Petropolis, Brazil. Design: Roberto Burle Marx and Haruyoshi Ono*

TOP MIDDLE: This European subtropical island garden can maintain plants from South Africa, Australia, as well as the Mediterannean. Even at the winter equinox over 300 plants can be found in flower here including aloes. *Abbey Garden, Tresco, Scilly Isles, UK. Design: Robert and Lucy Dorrien-Smith*

TOP RIGHT: In this steep hillside garden architectural plants such as bananas and hardy palms feature strongly. Azaleas, rhododendrons, and *Dicentra* (bleeding heart) add vibrant colour. *Seattle, WA, USA. Design: Owners, Lynn and Ralph Davis*

ABOVE: An example of an American exotic garden filled with lush and colourful plants of varying heights which shade a simple wooden-framed house. *Berkeley, CA, USA. Design: Former owners, Roger Raiche and David McRory*

RIGHT: A traditional Mongulu leaf house similar in style to those built by the indigenous people of the Cameroon rainforest, Africa. Planting includes banana, cassava, and maize. *"Green & Black's Rainforest Garden", RHS Chelsea Flower Show 2010. Design: Jane Owen with Ann-Marie Powell*

PAGE LEFT

TOP LEFT: A wooden pavilion sits amongst a created rainforest made of *Cyathea latebrosa, Ficus microcarpa* var. *nitida*, and *Rhapis multifida. The Tourism Malaysia Garden, RHS Chelsea Flower Show 2010. Design: David Cubero and James Wong*

TOP RIGHT: Caribbean courtyard garden planted with palms, *Allamanda violacea* (St. Phillips allamanda), and metrosideros. *Barbados. Design: Owner, Kevin Talma*

MIDDLE: This semi-tropical garden includes bromeliads, bananas, agave, and succulents. *The Teacup Garden, Chanticleer Garden, PA, USA. Design: Dan Benarcik*

BOTTOM: A natural pond surrounded by ferns, rustic wooden bridge, and gravel paths. *Speckhardt Mill, Hesse, Germany. Design: Owners, Siegfried and Rita Speckhardt*

RIGHT: Outdoor seating area in a shelter using bamboo, *Trachycarpus fortunei* (chusan palm, windmill palm), crocosmia, abutilon, and *Ginkgo biloba. Norwich, Norfolk, England. Design: Owner, Jon Kelf*

BELOW: Tropical garden with evergreen foliage plants including palms. Key design features include ceramic urns, a rill with stone bird fountain, a blue painted stone gateway into a courtyard, and columns of the house. *Baan Botanica, Bangkok, Thailand. Design: Owner, Bill Bensley*

ABOVE: Tropical garden with sweeping lawns, paths, lake, rainforest, and mountain backdrop. Planting includes flowering trees, shrubs, and canna. *Odette Monteiro Residence, Petropolis, Brazil. Design: Roberto Burle Marx*

ABOVE: A sturdy concrete table with wooden chairs sits shaded by a magnolia tree on a terrace of stone cobbles and grass overlooking a view to the Mediterranean. *Menton, Provence, France. Design: Owner, William Waterfield*

RIGHT: Brightly coloured mosaic is inlaid between the paving stones to get a Mediterranean effect. In late summer raised wooden beds are planted with dahlia, crocosmia, and hemerocallis flowers for additional colour. *Edinburgh, Scotland. Design: Owners, Raymond and Gail Paul*

PAGE RIGHT
TOP: To reflect the sun's rays steps and walls are painted white. Raised beds and containers are painted in pastel colours and planted with pelargoniums, *Dianthus* (pink), and a *Citrus sinensis* (orange) tree. *Cephalonia, Greece*

BELOW LEFT: A fountain is the focal point in this Morroccan-style courtyard, designed to represent the "elixir of life" in desert countries. The movement of the water also refreshes and circulates the air. Terracotta pots give architectural interest and are planted with *Phoenix canariensis*, citrus trees, and *Cyperus papyrus* whilst herbs and scented shrubs fill the air with fragrance. *SPANA's Courtyard Refuge, RHS Chelsea Flower Show 2008. Design: Chris O'Donoghue*

BELOW RIGHT: Patterned tiles feature here in this Mediterranean style courtyard garden. The warm colours of the terracotta tiled roof and red ochre 'rammed earth' walls add to the look. Key Mediterranean plants include *Astelia chatamica* 'Silver Spear', *Lavandula stoechas* (French lavender), *Cistus* (rock rose), *Acanthus spinosa* and *Eriobotrya japonica* (loquat). 'Casa Forte' courtyard garden at RHS Chelsea Flower Show 2007. Design: Stephen Firth and Nicola Ludlow-Monk.

PAGE LEFT

TOP: An historic tiled rooftop patio garden with a multitude of potted pelargoniums in terracotta pots designed to create a colourful display. *Casa de Pilatos, Seville, Spain*

BELOW LEFT: This famous conservatory is designed as a Mediterranean spring garden. A rill leading to a central pool is filled with *Cyperus papyrus* and forms the main focus around which grow cyclamen, narcissus, and *Hardenbergia violacea* 'Happy Wanderer'. *Mediterranean Garden, Longwood Gardens, PA, USA*

BELOW RIGHT: This sensuous garden is created with sumptuous plantings of old-fashioned shrub roses, peonies, *Foeniculum vulgare* (fennel), alliums, iris, dahlia, acanthus, and *Malus* (apple) tree in blossom. The simple architectural design includes elements such as Portland stone around a raised pool, lime-rendered walls, and sculptural seats. *The Lladro "Sensuality" Garden, RHS Chelsea Flower Show 2003. Design: Chris Moss and Fiona Lawrenson*

RIGHT: Here a typical French Mediterranean building is screened by a row of tall bamboo and given a splash of colour with pelargoniums. *Le Mas de la Brune, Eygalieres en Provence, France*

BELOW: A gravel path flanked by lavender leads to the door of this traditional pink-rendered house. Tamarisk shrubs soften the view. *Provence, France. Design: Owner, Alex Dingwall-Main*

ABOVE: This old Mini has been reused as a substantial plant container. The car is surrounded by lupins and ferns; windowboxes are planted with herbs. *"The Mini Garden", RHS Chelsea Flower Show 2003. Design: Sulis Garden Design*

LEFT: A chaotic metal trellis hung with garden tools, reclaimed household ornaments, and a planter with climbers. *Portland, OR, USA. Design: Owner, Nancy Goldman*

PAGE RIGHT
TOP LEFT: Recycled white goods planted with hanging ivy and drawers filled with wild flowers. *"Places of Change" Garden, Eden Project in partnership with Homes and Communities Agency, Communities and Local Government, Homeless Link, RHS Chelsea Flower Show 2010. Design: Paul Stone*

TOP MIDDLE: The wooden pergola in this recycled garden supports an old bicycle and chair, while a twisted cane support has been built below for a container of succulents. *Portland, OR, USA. Design: Owner, Nancy Goldman*

BOTTOM LEFT: A recycled rubber tyre has been turned into an urn and then filled with old cutlery to create a shell-like appearance. *Berkeley, CA, USA. Design: Owner, Marcia Donahue*

BOTTOM MIDDLE: Old motorbike tyres are used as containers planted with *Zantedeschia schwarzwalder* and surrounded by *Ophiopogon planiscapus* 'Nigrescens' (black lilyturf). *"The Ace of Spades" Garden, RHS Chelsea Flower Show 2009. Design: David Domoney*

TOP: This variegated standard *Ilex* (holly) tree is planted in a rusted metal container with recycled rubber chipping used as a mulch. *Hertfordshire, England. Design: Owner, Kim Wilde*

ABOVE: Recycled tyres have been painted to create a colourful container planted with sweetcorn and potatoes. *"Recycle Re-use and Relax" Garden, Gardening Scotland, Edinburgh. Design: Perennial and Oatridge College*

ABOVE: This homemade greenhouse has been created from recycled plastic bottles strung together on bamboo canes. *"Places of Change" Garden by the Eden Project, RHS Chelsea Flower Show 2010. Design: Paul Stone*

FAR LEFT: This greenhouse uses recycled plastic water bottles slotted together for the walls. Bamboo canes are placed to provide support for the young tomato plants. *Suntrap Garden, Edinburgh, Scotland. Design: Suntrap Garden*

LEFT: Recycled plastic water bottles are used here as protection for young lettuces. The lids are left off for ventilation. *Ayrshire, Scotland. Design: Andrea Currie*

ABOVE: This screen is decorated with reclaimed painted doors and windows making an interesting backdrop for planting. It also allows light and views through the fence. *Portland, OR, USA. Design: Owner, Nancy Goldman*

ABOVE: A recycled paving slab of roughcast concrete makes a vertical wall for this raised bed. *Orinda, CA, USA. Design: Topher Delaney*

LEFT: A tree doubles as a message board with notes hung on the branches. *"Places of Change" Garden by the Eden Project, RHS Chelsea Flower Show 2010. Design: Paul Stone*

LEFT: This small back garden planted with spring bulbs, shrubs, and ornamental grasses is enhanced by uplighters. *Delft, Holland. Design: Lisa Zago-Bücher*

BELOW LEFT: Lights in the borders of this contemporary kitchen garden extend the day time. The light accentuates patterns made by the foliage of a young olive tree on the yellow painted wall. Sage and rosemary fill the border edges by the concrete seating. *WXD Cafe, Crouch End, London. Design: Dan Pearson and Steve Bradley*

PAGE RIGHT
ABOVE LEFT: A warm and inviting atmosphere is created around this swimming pool and deck by light shining through a combination of leafy trees and plants. *Cancer Research UK Garden, RHS Chelsea Flower Show 2006. Design: Andy Sturgeon*

ABOVE RIGHT: Stripey shadows on the smooth boulders are created by lighting the architectural foliage of the phormiums in this contemporary coastal garden. *Tregony, Cornwall, England. Design: David Buurma*

RIGHT: Uplighters feature in this contemporary coastal garden and are enhanced by being reflected in the water feature. *Tregony, Cornwall, England. Design: David Buurma*

FAR RIGHT: A small downlighter picks up the texture of the seedheads of *Pennisetum* (fountain grass) and the colour of a pink rose. *Evening Island, Chicago Botanic Garden, USA. Design: Lisa E. Delplace, Oehme, van Sweden*

ABOVE: Glass screens diffuse the light placed in the ground cover of the driveway and illuminate the tree above in this iconic modernist garden. Photographed 1/08/2008. *Indianapolis Museum of Art, Miller House and Garden, Columbus, IN, USA. Design: Dan Kiley*

LEFT: Light shines on a gently undulating path enhancing the gradient in this example of precision landscape architecture. In the background the bronze sculpture, *5 Dancing Figures* by Magdalena Abakanowicz, is silhouetted against the trees behind. *Jacquie and Bennett Dorrance Sculpture Garden, Phoenix Art Museum, Phoenix, AZ, USA. Design: Reed Hilderbrand*

ABOVE: Translucent white material above a rusted steel wall diffuses light to create a gentle ambience in this garden. Scented *Trachelospermum jasminoides* (star jasmine) climbs beside it and a row of *Tulbaghia violacea* is planted below. *Orinda, CA, USA. Design: Topher Delaney*

TOP RIGHT: Light shines through a sculptural form made from reclaimed glass, lighting a dark corner in this garden made of recycled materials. *Orinda, CA, USA. Design: Topher Delaney*

RIGHT: Temporary lighting in glass jars on each step guides guests to an evening eating area. *Chanticleer Garden, PA, USA. Lighting design: "Simple"*

LEFT TOP: A small formal rose garden uses raised wooden edged beds to display tree roses. *The Donnell Garden, Sonoma, CA, USA. Design: Thomas Church, Lawrence Halprin, and George Rockrise*

LEFT MIDDLE: Modern-looking circular garden with a border filled with red roses for colour. *"L'Oeuvre au Rouge", Le Jardin de l'Alchimiste, Eygalieres en Provence, France. Design: Arnaud Maurières and Eric Ossart*

LEFT: This grand circular arbour is covered with climbing *Rosa* 'American Pillar'. *Longwood Gardens, PA, USA*

ABOVE: A scented climbing rose grows up the wall of the porch in this cottage garden. *Wiltshire, England. Design: Owner, Victoria Kerr*

ABOVE RIGHT: Decorative rose-painted patio tiles add extra femininity to this courtyard garden with climbing roses amongst topiary shapes. *"Wherefore Art Thou?", RHS Chelsea Flower Show 2002. Design: Sarah Brodie and Faith Dewhurst*

RIGHT: Fragrance and shade are offered to the visitor walking through this arbour heavy with climbing roses. *The Low Gardens, Generalife, The Alhambra, Granada, Spain*

ABOVE: Lines of *Festuca glauca* (blue fescue) across a large surface make a dramatic impact in this display garden. *Cornerstone Festival of Gardens, Sonoma, CA, USA. Design: Lutsko Associates*

LEFT: The grey-green foliage of *Cynara cardunculus* (cardoon) complements the sea of gentle pink-flowered Japanese anemones in this country garden. *Shropshire, England. Design: Jenny Goodrich*

ABOVE: Layers of plants provide colour and texture. Above is *Acer palmatum* (Japanese maple), *Cyperus papyrus*, and *Trachycarpus fortunei*, while underneath ferns include *Asplenium scolopendrium* which grows around the small pool. *Lamorran House Gardens, Cornwall, England. Design: Owner, Robert Dudley-Cooke*

RIGHT: *Echinocactus grusonii* (golden barrel cactus) are used as a bold statement in this desert garden. Opuntia and flowering yuccas provide the backdrop. *Walnut Creek, CA, USA. Design: Owner, Ruth Bancroft*

ABOVE: Here a swathe of restios hold centre stage in this exposed clifftop plantsman's garden. *Indianola, WA, USA. Design: Owners, Daniel J. Hinkley and Robert Jones*

LEFT: *Onopordum acanthium* (Scotch thistle) steals the limelight in this country garden border – its silver-grey stems and foliage contrast beautifully against the *Cotinus coggygria* (smokebush). *Hampshire, England. Design: Owner, Mrs. J. Budden*

FOLLOWING PAGE: These drought-tolerant plants co-exist happily on a dry slope in this Mediterranean-style coastal terrace. Architectural plants include agave, aeonium, and *Trachycarpus fortunei* (chusan palm, windmill palm). *Lamorran House Gardens, Cornwall, England. Design: Owner, Robert Dudley-Cooke*

ABOVE :
Coloured walls with muted tones provide a gently contrasting backdrop to native Arizona succulents and cacti. *Paradise Valley, AZ, USA. Design: Steve Martino*

ABOVE MIDDLE:
A tall spindly cactus mirrors the form of the rebar rods in the concrete wall behind in this contemporary desert garden. *Paradise Valley, AZ, USA. Design: Steve Martino*

ABOVE RIGHT:
A red rendered wall provides the perfect contrasting backdrop for silver-blue agaves. *Paradise Valley, AZ, USA. Design: Steve Martino*

RIGHT: Back lighting enhances the texture of the spines of *Opuntia erinacea* var. *ursina* and the colour of *Callindra eriophylla. Walnut Creek, CA, USA. Design: Ruth Bancroft*

GARDENS

Brazil
Sítio Roberto Burle Marx
Estrada da Barra de Guaratiba,
2019, Barra de Guaratiba,
Rio de Janeiro
portal.iphan.gov.br

Canada
Jardin de Métis/Reford Gardens
220, Route 132, Grand-Métis
(Québec) GOJ 1ZO
www.jardinsdemetis.com

England
Abbey House Gardens
Malmesbury, Wiltshire SN16 9AS
www.abbeyhousegardens.co.uk

Apple Court
Hordle Lane, Hordle, Lymington,
Hampshire SO41 0HU
www.applecourt.com

Bonython Estate Gardens
Bonython Estate, Cury Cross Lanes,
Helston, Cornwall TR12 7BA
www.bonythonmanor.co.uk

Columbine Hall
Stowupland, Stowmarket,
Suffolk IP14 4AT
www.columbinehall.co.uk

The Dalemain Estate
Dalemain, Penrith,
Cumbria CA11 0HB
www.dalemain.com

East Ruston Old Vicarage
East Ruston, Norfolk NR12 9HN
www.ngs.org.uk/gardens/gardenfinder

The Eden Project
Bodelva, Cornwall PL24 2SG
www.edenproject.com

Great Dixter
High Park Close, Northiam, Rye,
East Sussex TN31 6PH
www.greatdixter.co.uk/gardens.htm

Great Fosters Hotel
Stroude Road, Egham, Surrey
TW20 9UR
www.greatfosters.co.uk

Hampton Court Palace
East Molesey, Surrey KT8 9AU
www.hrp.org.uk/hamptoncourtpalace

Hestercombe Gardens
Cheddon Fitzpaine, Taunton,
Somerset TA2 7LG
www.hestercombe.com

Hidcote Manor
Hidcote Bartrim, near Chipping
Campden, Gloucestershire GL55
6LR
www.nationaltrust.org.uk/main/
w-hidcote.htm

Kelmarsh Hall and Gardens
Kelmarsh, Northampton NN6 9LY
www.kelmarsh.com

Lady Farm
Lady Farm Gardens, Chelwood,
Somerse BS39 4NN
www.ladyfarm.com

Lamorran House Gardens
Lamorran House, Upper Castle
Road, St. Mawes, Cornwall TR2 5BZ
www.lamorrangardens.co.uk

Levens Hall and Gardens
Kendal, Cumbria LA8 0PD
www.levenshall.co.uk

Misarden Park Gardens
Miserden Estate, Near Stroud,
Gloucestershire GL6 7AJ
www.misardenpark.co.uk

Norfolk Lavender Company
Caley Mill, Lynn Road, Heacham,
King's Lynn, Norfolk PE31 7JE
www.norfolk-lavender.co.uk

Royal Botanic Gardens, Kew
Kew, Richmond, Surrey TW9 3AB
www.kew.org

Scampston Hall
Malton, North Yorkshire YO17 8NG
www.scampston.co.uk

Sissinghurst
Biddenden Road, near Cranbrook,
Kent TN17 2AB
www.nationaltrust.org.uk/main/
w-sissinghurst-castle/

Summerdale Garden
Summerdale House, Cow Brow,
Lupton, Carnforth LA6 1PE
www.summerdalegardenplants.co.uk

Titsey Place and Gardens
Oxted, Surrey
www.titsey.org

Tresco Abbey Garden
Tresco, Isles of Scilly TR24 0QQ
www.tresco.co.uk

Wakehurst Place
Ardingly, Haywards Heath, West
Sussex RH17 6TN
www.nationaltrust.org.uk/main/w-
wakehurstplace

RHS Wisley
Woking, Surrey GU23 6QB
www.rhs.org.uk/wisley

France
Le Jardin de l'Alchimiste
Le Mas de la Brune, 13810
Eygalieres
www.jardin-alchimiste.com

Jardin Atlantique
Gare Montparnasse, 75015 Paris

La Bambouseraie
Domaine de Prafrance, 30140
Générargues
www.bambouseraie.com

Parc André Citroën
Quai André-Citroën, Ile-de-France,
75015 Paris

Château de Villandry
3 Rue Principale, 37510 Villandry
www.chateauvillandry.fr

Germany
Grugapark Essen
Virchowstraße 167a, 45147 Essen
www.grugapark.de/im-park.html

Hermannshof
Babostraße 5, 69469 Weinheim
www.sichtungsgarten-
hermannshof.de/index.php

Westpark
Westendstrasse, Munich
www.gardenvisit.com/garden/
west_park_munich

Holland
Keukenhof
Keukenhof, near Lisse
www.keukenhof.nl

Ireland
June Blake's Garden
Tinode, Blessington, Co. Wicklow
www.juneblake.ie

The Dillon Garden
45 Sandford Road, Ranelagh, Dublin 6
www.dillongarden.com

Hunting Brook Gardens
Hunting Brook, Lamb Hill,
Blessington, Co. Wicklow, Ireland
www.huntingbrook.com

Japan
Showa Kinen Park
3173 Midori-cho, Tachikawa City,
Tokyo 190-8530
www.showakinenpark.go.jp

Northern Ireland
Portaferry Road, Newtownards,
County Down, BT22 2AD
beta.nationaltrust.org.uk/mount-
stewart

Scotland
Ascog Hall Gardens
Ascog Hall, Scog, Isle of Bute PA20
9EU
www.ascoghallfernery.co.uk

Cambo Gardens
Cambo House, Kingsbarns, St.
Andrews, Fife KY16 8QD
www.camboestate.com/gardens

Crathes Castle
Banchory, Aberdeen and Grampian
AB31 5QJ
www.nts.org.uk/Property/20

Edzell Castle and Gardens
Perthshire, Kinross and Angus,
DD9 7UE

The Hidden Gardens
25A Albert Drive, Glasgow G41 2PE
www.thehiddengardens.org.uk

Inverewe Garden and Estate
Poolewe, Ross-shire, IV22 2LG
www.nts.org.uk/Property/36

**Lip na Cloiche Garden and
Nursery**
Ballygown, Ulva Ferry, Isle of Mull,
Argyll PA73 6LU
www.lipnacloiche.co.uk

Mount Stuart
Mount Stuart,
Isle of Bute PA20 9LR
www.mountstuart.com

Shepherd House Garden
Inveresk, Midlothian, EH21 7TH
www.shepherdhousegarden.co.uk

Spain
La Alhambra
Granada, Andalusia
www.turgranada.es

Casa de Pilatos
Plaza de Pilatos 1, Seville, Spain
www.fundacionmedinaceli.org

Madeira Botanical Gardens
Madeira
www.madeira-web.com/PagesUK/
botanical.html

Sweden
The Japanese Garden
Ronneby Brunnspark
www.ronneby.se

USA
**The Arnold Arboretum of Harvard
University**
125 Arborway,
Boston, MA 02130-3500
arboretum.harvard.edu

**Beatrix Farrand Garden at
Bellefield**
4097 Albany Post Road,
Hyde Park, NY 12538
www.beatrixfarrandgarden.org

Biltmore Estate
1 Lodge Street,
Asheville, NC 28803
www.biltmore.com

The Bloedel Reserve
7571 N.E. Dolphin Drive,
Bainbridge Island, WA 98110
www.bloedelreserve.org

Brooklyn Botanic Garden
1000 Washington Ave,
Brooklyn, NY 11225
www.bbg.org

Chanticleer Garden
788 Church Road, Wayne, PA 19087
www.chanticleergarden.org

Chicago Botanic Garden
1000 Lake Cook Road,
Glencoe, IL 60022
www.chicagobotanic.org

Cornerstone Gardens
Cornerstone Sonoma, 23570 Arnold
Dr, Sonoma, CA 95476
www.cornerstonegardens.com

Denver Botanic Gardens
1007 York Street, Denver, CO 80206
www.botanicgardens.org

Dumbarton Oaks
1703 32nd Street, NW,
Washington, DC 20007
www.doaks.or

Fairchild Tropical Garden
10901 Old Cutler Road,
Miami, FL 33156
www.ftg.org

Garden in the Woods
180 Hemenway Road,
Framingham, MA 01701-2699
www.newenglandwild.org

Huntington Botanic Gardens
1151 Oxford Road,
San Marino, CA 91108
www.huntington.org

**Indianapolis Museum of Art
Miller House and Garden**
Columbus Area Visitors Center, 506
Fifth Street, Columbus, IN 47201
www.imamuseum.org

J.C. Raulston Arboretum
Department of Horticultural
Science, NC State University,
Campus Box 7522,
Raleigh, NC 27695-7522
www.ncsu.edu/jcraulstonarboretum

Juntunen Farm and Gardens
18091 Burkland Road,
Mount Vernon, WA 98274
juntunengardens.com

Keller Fountain Park
SW 3rd Ave & Clay St,
Portland, OR 97255

**Lady Bird Johnson Wildflower
Center**
4801 La Crosse Avenue,
Austin, TX 78739
www.wildflower.org

GARDEN CENTRES

Lan Su Chinese Garden
NW 3rd & Everett,
Portland, OR 97209
www.portlandchinesegarden.org

Longhouse Reserve
133 Hands Creek Road,
East Hampton, NY 11937
longhouse.org

Longwood Gardens
1001 Longwood Road,
Kennett Square, PA 19348
www.longwoodgardens.org

Lotusland
695 Ashley Road
Santa Barbara, CA 93108-1059
www.lotusland.org/

Lurie Garden
Millenium Park, Grant Park, Chicago, IL
www.millenniumpark.org

Madoo Conservancy
618 Sagg Main Street, Sagaponack, NY 11962
www.madoo.org

Missouri Botanic Garden
4344 Shaw Blvd., St. Louis, MO 63110
www.mobot.org

Monticello
931 Thomas Jefferson Parkway,
Charlottesville, VA 22902
www.monticello.org

Naumkeag
5 Prospect Hill Road
Stockbridge, MA 01262
www.thetrustees.org/places-to-
visit/berkshires/naumkeag.html

New York Botanical Garden
Bronx River Parkway at Fordham Road,
Bronx, NY 10458
www.nybg.org

The Noguchi Museum
32-37 Vernon Boulevard,
Long Island City, NY 11106
www.noguchi.org

Peconic Land Trust Bridge Gardens
36 Mitchells Lane, Bridgehampton, NY 11932
www.peconiclandtrust.org

Phipps Conservatory
1 Schenley Park, Pittsburgh, PA 15213
www.phipps.conservatory.org

Phoenix Art Museum
McDowell Road & Central Avenue, 1625 N.
Central Avenue, Phoenix, AZ 85004
www.phxart.org

Portland Japanese Garden
611 SW Kingston Ave, Portland, OR, 97205
japanesegarden.com

The Ruth Bancroft Garden
1552 Bancroft Road, Walnut Creek, CA 94598
www.ruthbancroftgarden.org

Santa Barbara Botanic Garden
1212 Mission Canyon Road,
Santa Barbara, CA 93105
www.sbbg.org

Stonecrop Garden
81 Stonecrop Lane,
Cold Spring, NY 10516
www.stonecrop.org

Wave Hill
West 249th St. and Independence Ave.,
Bronx, NY 10471
www.wavehill.org

Ireland
Avoca at Mount Usher Gardens
Ashford, County Wicklow
www.mountushergardens.ie

DYG
www.dyg.ie

UK
Baileys Home and Garden
Whitecross Farm, Bridstow HR9 6JU
www.baileyshomeandgarden.com

Beth Chatto Gardens
Elmstead Market, Colchester, Essex CO7 7DB
www.bethchatto.co.uk

Clifton Nurseries
5A, Clifton Villas, London W9 2PH
www.clifton.co.uk

Daylesford Farmshop & Café
Daylesford, Gloucestershire GL56 0YG

Denmans Garden
Denmans Lane, Fontwell,
West Sussex BN18 0SU
www.denmans-garden.co.uk

Larch Cottage Nurseries
Melkinthorpe, Penrith, Cumbria CA10 2DR
www.larchcottage.co.uk

Marchants Hardy Plants
2 Marchants Cottages, Mill Lane, Laughton,
East Sussex BN8 6AJ
www.marchantshardyplants.co.uk

Petersham Nurseries
Church Lane, off Petersham Road, Richmond,
Surrey TW10 7AG
www.petershamnurseries.com

Waddesdon Plant & Garden Centre
Queen Street, Waddesdon, Bucks HP18 0JW
www.clifton.co.uk

USA
Annie's Annuals & Perennials
801 Chesley Avenue, Richmond, CA 94801
www.anniesannuals.com

Avant Gardens
710 High Hill Road, Dartmouth, MA 02747
www.avantgardensne.com

Cottage Gardens
6967 Rte 111, Piasa, IL 62079
www.cottgardens.com

Emory Knoll Farms Inc.
3410 Ady Road, Street, MD 21154
www.greenroofplants.com

Flora Grubb Gardens
1634 Jerrold Avenue,
San Francisco, CA 94131
www.floragrubb.com

Niche Gardens
1111 Dawson Road, Chapel Hill, NC 27516
www.nichegardens.com

Northwind Perennial Farm
7047 Hospital Road, Burlington, WI 53105
northwindperennialfarm.com

Perennial Pleasures
63 Brickhouse Road,
East Hardwick, VT 05836
www.perennialpleasures.net

**Plant Delights Nursery at Juniper Level
Botanic Gardens**
9241 Sauls Road, Raleigh, NC 27603
www.plantdelights.com

Santa Fe Greenhouses
2904 Rufina Street, Santa Fe, NM 87507
www.santafegreenhouses.com

Terrain at Styers
914 Baltimore Pike, Glen Mills, PA 19342
styers.shopterrain.com

GARDEN FESTIVALS

Canada
International Garden Festival
Grand-Métis, Gaspésie, Québec
www.jardinsdemetis.com

France
Chaumont-sur-Loire Garden Festival
Chaumont-sur-Loire
www.domaine-chaumont.fr

Jardins, Jardin
Paris
www.jardinsjardin.com

Holland
Floriade
World Horticultural Expo, Venlo
www.floriade.com

UK
BBC Gardeners' World Live
NEC, Birmingham
www.bbcgardenersworldlive.com

Cottesbrooke Plant Finders Fair
Cottesbrooke Hall, Northampton
www.cottesbrookehall.co.uk

Gardening Scotland
The Royal Highland Centre,
Ingliston, Edinburgh
www.gardeningscotland.com

Malvern Autumn Show
Three Counties Showground, Malvern
www.threecounties.co.uk/malvernautumn/

RHS Chelsea Flower Show
Royal Hospital, Chelsea, London
www.rhs.org.uk

RHS Flower Show Tatton Park
Tatton Park, Knutsford, Cheshire
www.rhs.org.uk

RHS Hampton Court Palace Flower Show
Hampton Court Palace, Surrey
www.rhs.org.uk

**The Royal Bath and West National
Gardening Show**
Shepton Mallet, Somerset
ww.bathandwest.com/national-gardening/95/

USA
Garden Open Days
The Garden Conservancy, P.O. Box 219,
Cold Spring, NY 10516
www.gardenconservancy.org

Garden Walk
P.O.Box 161, Buffalo, NY 14207
gardenwalkbuffalo.com

Lilac Festival
Rochester, NY
www.lilacfestival.com

Philadelphia International Flower Show
Philadelphia, PA
www.theflowershow.com

DESIGNERS

Acres Wild
West Sussex, UK
www.acreswild.co.uk

Alexander-Sinclair, James
Towcester, Northamptonshire, UK
www.blackpitts.co.uk

Bensley, Bill (Bensley Design Studios)
Bangkok, Thailand
www.bensley.com

Bradley-Hole, Christopher
Richmond, Surrey, UK
www.christopherbradley-hole.co.uk

Brodie, Sarah and Dewhurst, Faith (Beyond Eden)
London, UK
www.beyondeden.co.uk

Buurma, David (Mor Design)
Falmouth, Cornwall, UK
www.mor-design.co.uk

Caligari, Chris (Chris Caligari Landscapes)
Worcester, UK
www.chriscaligari.com

Cao, Andy and Perrot, Xavier (Cao Perrot Studio)
Los Angeles, USA/Paris, France
www.caoperrotstudio.com

City Design Cooperative
Glasgow, Scotland, UK
www.citydesign.coop

Clément, Gilles
France
www.gillesclement.com

Cubero, David and Wong, James (Amphibian Designs)
London, UK
www.amphibiandesigns.com

Dale Loth Architects
London, UK
www.dalelotharchitects.ltd.uk

Darke, Rick
Landenberg, PA, USA
www.rickdarke.com

De la Fleur, Marcus
Chicago, IL, USA
www.delafleur.com

Del Buono, Tommaso and Gazerwitz, Paul (del Buono Gazerwitz Landscape Architecture)
London, UK
www.delbuono-gazerwitz.co.uk

Delaney, Topher (SEAM Studio)
San Francisco, CA, USA
www.tdelaney.com

Dingwall-Main, Alex
West Sussex, UK
www.alexdingwallmain.com

Domoney, David
UK
www.daviddomoney.com

Dooley, Helen and James (Helen Dooley Design)
Steneby, Sweden
www.hdgardens.com

Dowle, Julian (Julian Dowle Partnership)
Newent, Gloucestershire, UK
www.juliandowle.co.uk

Dunstan, Jamie (Gardener's Boutique)
South Yorkshire, UK
www.psinursery.co.uk

Eberle, Sarah (Sarah Eberle Landscape Design)
Hampshire, UK
www.saraheberle.com

Forristt, Cevan (Cevan Forristt Landscape Design)
San Jose, CA, USA
www.forristt.com

Fox, Patricia
Hatfield Heath, Hertfordshire, UK
www.aralia.org.uk

Fox, Patricia (Aralia Garden Design & Build)
Bishop's Stortford, Hertfordshire, UK
www.aralia.org.uk

Gavin, Diarmuid (Diarmund Gavin Designs)
London, UK
www.diarmuidgavindesigns.co.uk

Giubbilei, Luciano
London, UK
www.lucianogiubbilei.com

Gough, Graham & Goffin, Lucy
Lewes, East Sussex, UK
www.marchantshardyplants.co.uk

Green, Naila
Dawlish, Devon, UK
nailagreengardendesign.co.uk

Greene, Isabelle (Isabelle Greene & Associates)
Santa Barbara, CA, USA
www.isabellegreene.com

Gregory, Mark (Landform Consultants)
Surrey, UK
www.landformconsultants.co.uk

Guinness, Bunny
Peterborough, Cambridgeshire, UK
www.bunnyguinness.com

Gustafson, Kathryn
Seattle, WA, USA
www.kathryngustafson.com

Heatherington, Catherine
London, UK
www.chdesigns.co.uk

Hempel, Anouska (Anouska Hempel Design)
London, UK
www.anouskahempeldesign.com

Heywood, Tony
London, UK
www.conceptualgardens.co.uk

Hinkley, Daniel J.
Indianola, WA, USA
www.danielhinkley.com

Hoblyn, Thomas
Bury St Edmonds, Suffolk, UK
new.thomashoblyn.com

Hogan, Sean
Portland, OR, USA
www.cistus.com

Hudson, Jane & De Maeijer, Erik (Hudson De Maeijer)
London, UK
www.janehudson.co.uk

Ingberg, Hal (Hal Ingberg Architecte)
Montréal, Canada
www.halingberg.com

Jencks, Charles
Scotland, UK
www.charlesjencks.com

Jones, Robert
Reading, UK
www.gardendesignco.co.uk

Kingsbury, Noel
Herefordshire, UK
www.noelkingsbury.com

Land Use Consultants
London, UK
www.landuse.co.uk

Latham, Bob (Posh Gardens)
Clevedon, Somerset, UK
www.poshgardens.com

Lawrenson, Fiona and Moss, Chris (Fiona Lawrenson Garden Design)
Haslemere, Surrey, UK
www.fionalawrenson.com

Lennox-Boyd, Arabella
London, UK
www.arabellalennoxboyd.com

Lisa E. Delpace (see van Sweden)

Lloyd-Morgan, Daniel
London, UK
www.dlmgardendesign.co.uk

Lutsko Associates
San Francisco, CA, USA
www.lutskoassociates.com

Mackenzie Panizzon, Lucy
Isle of Mull, Scotland, UK
www.lipnacloiche.co.uk

Marston and Langinger
London, UK
www.marston-and-langinger.com

Martin, Paul (Paul Martin Designs)
Dublin, Ireland
paulmartindesigns.com

Martino, Steve (Steve Martino & Associates)
Phoenix, AZ, USA
www.stevemartino.net

Maurières, Arnaud and Ossart, Eric
France
www.maurieres-ossart.com

Maynard, Arne
London, UK
www.arne-maynard.com

McBeath, Colin
Ceres, Fife, Scotland, UK
www.creatingeden.co.uk

McCrory, David & Raiche, Roger (Planet Horticulture)
Califorinia, USA
www.planethorticulture.com

McCulloch, Carol Gallagher (Carol Gallagher McCulloch Landscape Designs)
Dunblane, UK
www.cgmgardendesigns.co.uk

Nordfjell, Ulf
Stockholm, Sweden
www.nordfjellcollection.se

nva organisation
Glasgow, Scotland, UK
www.nva.org.uk

O'Donoghue, Chris
Hastings, East Sussex, UK
www.chrisodonoghue.co.uk

Onion Flats
Philadelphia, PA, USA
www.onionflats.com

Oudolf, Piet
Hummelo, The Netherlands
www.oudolf.com

Pawson, John
London, UK
www.johnpawson.com

Pearson, Dan (Dan Pearson Studio)
London, UK
www.danpearsonstudio.com

Powell, Ann-Marie
West Sussex, UK
www.ann-mariepowell.com

Price, Sarah
London, UK
sarahpricelandscapes.com

Redmore, David
Lancaster, Lancashire, UK
www.gardenandlandscapedesign.co.uk

Reed Hilderbrand
Watertown, MA, USA
www.reedhilderbrand.com

Reynolds, Mary
Ireland
www.maryreynoldsdesigns.com

Roofscapes Inc.
Philadelphia, PA, USA
www.roofmeadow.com

Rowe, Charlotte
London, UK
www.charlotterowe.com

Sasaki, Yoji (Ohtori Associates)
Osaka, Japan
www.ohtori-c.com

Schwartz, Martha
Cambridge, MA, USA
www.marthaschwartz.com

Shaw, Carol
Renfrewshire, Scotland, UK
www.cshawgardendesign.com

Silva, Roberto
London, UK
www.silvalandscapes.com

Snodgrass, Ed (Green Roof Plants)
Maryland, USA
www.greenroofplants.com

Stone, Paul
Falmouth, Cornwall, UK
www.paulstonegardens.co.uk

Stoss Landscape Urbanism
Boston, MA, USA
www.stoss.net

Stuart-Smith, Tom
London, UK
www.tomstuartsmith.co.uk

Stubbs, Jacqui (Remarkable Gardens)
Arrowtown, New Zealand
www.remarkablegardens.co.nz

Sturgeon, Andy
Brighton, UK
www.andysturgeon.com

Swift, Joe
London, UK
www.joeswift.co.uk

Takano, Fumiaki
Sapporo, Hokkaido, Japan
www.tlp.co.jp

Talma, Kevin (Talma Mill Studios)
Barbados
talmamillstudios.com

Tollemache, Xa
Stowmarket, Suffolk, UK
www.xa-tollemache.co.uk

van der Kloet, Jacqueline
Weesp, The Netherlands
www.theetuin.nl

van Sweden, James (Oehme, van Sweden & Associates)
Washington DC, USA
www.ovsla.com

Vlan Paysages
Montréal, Canada
www.vlanpaysages.ca

Wear, Alison (Alison Wear Garden Design)
London, UK
www.alisonwear.com

West, Cleve (Cleve West Landscape Design)
Hampton Wick, Surrey, UK
www.clevewest.com

White, Susie
Northumberland, UK
www.susie-white.co.uk

Wilkie, Kim (Kim Wilkie Associates)
Richmond, Surrey, UK
www.kimwilkie.com

Woodhams, Stephen
London, UK
www.woodhams.co.uk

INDEX

Page numbers in *italics* refer to picture captions